Uffe Andersen
Gunnar Pall Thorisson
Björn Gunnar Karlsson

Strategic Budgeting

A Computer Program for Strategic Budgeting and Performance Assessment

Copenhagen Business School Press
HANDELSHØJSKOLENS FORLAG

1. edition, 2. impression 2001

Printed in Denmark by Reproset, Copenhagen
ISBN 87-630-00008-8

Distribution:

Scandinavia
DBK, Siljangade 2-8, P.O. Box 1731
DK-2300 Copenhagen S, Denmark
phone: +45 3269 7788, fax: +45 3269 7789

North America
Copenhagen Business School Press
Books International Inc.
P.O. Box 605
Herndon, VA 20172-0605, USA
phone: +1 703 661 1500, fax: +1 703 661 1501

Rest of the World
Marston Book Services, P.O. Box 269
Abingdon, Oxfordshire, OX14 4YN, UK
phone: +44 (0) 1235 465500, fax: +44 (0) 1235 465555
E-mail Direct Customers: direct.order@marston.co.uk
E-mail Booksellers: trade.order@marston.co.uk

Table of Contents

Part II

User´s Guide to the Computer Models

Foreword

Through our work as consultants in the fields of strategic management and information technology, we have found that in many companies there is a gap between basic strategic and financial management theories, on the one hand, and company processes and procedures on the other. Managers do not apply modern planning and control methods and tools in their operations. Our aim is to address this problem by transforming professional management techniques and analytical methods into useful and practical tools for the ordinary business manager.

The accompanying computer models are intended as aids to strategic budgeting, performance management and prediction of the future economic performance of companies. Every attempt has been made to keep the models simple and accessible.

We believe that the models can stimulate creative discussions and raise management efficiency.

The Equity Ratio is the focal point of this book. We believe that in order to secure the long-range survival of a company it is necessary to plan and control the parallel trends regarding profit and assets. This means that companies should pay more attention to balance-sheet items than they normally do. Actually, long-range survival is far more closely linked to the relative sizes of assets and liabilities than to profit alone. The Equity Ratio is a snapshot of the balance, and indicates the leverage of the company. This simple ratio tells us how well prepared the company is to deal with its future development. The Equity Ratio should therefore be one of the key elements in long-range planning, budgeting and performance assessment.

The book contains suggestions, tools and early-warning systems that make such planning and control possible.

We hope that it will prove useful and stimulate the professional analysis of financial indicators in management.

Finally, we should like to thank all those who helped with their constructive criticisms and helpful suggestions and with developing the computer models.

Uffe Andersen
Gunnar Pall Thorisson
Björn Gunnar Karlsson

Introduction

In this book we discuss how financial indicators of the performance and financial standing of the company can be used in a simple way for setting targets, monitoring results and predicting future trends.

Based on Microsoft Excel, the computer models calculate all the main financial indicators and present financial data graphically. All that is needed is to put in a few figures on operations and financial standing, and the processing can be left to the models. This makes it possible for managers to concentrate on the analysis and interpretation of the data, whether they are drawing up business plans or reviewing performance figures.

The book discusses the material on a theoretical basis, but we have attempted to avoid theoretical speculations which have no direct practical value.

We use the term "indicators" to refer to indices of profitability, financial strength and many other factors which are generally not directly expressed in accounts, annual reports or budgets. Generally, they take the form of ratios obtained by dividing one operational figure by another. Various ordinary financial ratios such as Return on Equity, the Current Ratio and Asset Turnover are used all over the world to measure companies' performance. One indicator by itself does not tell the whole story, but together they can reveal the strengths and weaknesses of the company and its managers.

Experience shows that in practice, business plans are often of little benefit as managerial tools. Planning tends to become an annual routine, based on the use of the previous year's plan. Such business plans do not encourage people to make new efforts. The type of business plan that is useful as a managerial tool is based on creative strategic planning, blending together targeting and down-to-earth reality.

Indicators are not only of use to managers engaged in drawing up business plans and performance management. Company owners who are not involved in day-to-day operations can use indicators to assess the results achieved by professional managers, and investors on the stock exchange can use them to assess investment options. Other market players should be able to make use of indicators to evaluate companies' results and future performance.

The book is divided into two main parts. Part I consists of four chapters and examines ratio analysis as a managerial tool.

Chapter 1 discusses planning and business performance in general terms and introduces a model showing the connection between various concepts in business management, giving the reader an overview of how financial indicators can be used in management and competitive analysis.

Chapter 2 contains a description of ratios indicating returns and corporate financial strength.

In Chapter 3 we discuss the Equity Ratio in more detail. We argue that the Equity Ratio should be considered a key issue in Strategic Management. We then discuss how the Equity Ratio can be managed and controlled.

Chapter 4 examines the possibility of turning budgets into powerful strategic tools, first with the accent on introducing ideas for using ratios and targets in short-term traditional budgeting, and then by presenting a framework for long-range strategic budgeting based on the parameters which directly affect the development of the Equity Ratio.

Part II, consisting of three chapters, is a user guide describing and explaining the use of the accompanying computer models.

Chapter 5 contains a general discussion of the models. It explains general features of the models and how they are structured and related to each other.

Chapter 6 explains in more detail the various models for Operational Ratio Analysis. First, the chapter discusses and explains Annual Ratio Analysis by quarters and months, and then attention is given to Ratio Analysis of Trends, i.e., ratio analysis of the annual accounts in order to monitor trends in key ratios from one year to the next. Finally, the chapter describes the DuPont Model and the use of graphs and charts for the presentation of data. The DuPont Model is a powerful analytical tool which shows the causal connection between operational and Balance-Sheet figures and return ratios.

Chapter 7 examines models for Strategic Ratio Analysis. These models calculate, e.g., future values of key ratios, based on assumptions of the strategic situation and possible future scenarios.

Two appendices follow at the end of the book. Appendix A describes the installation and setup procedure for the models and Appendix B explains how to change the standard graph layouts and how to develop customised ratios.

Part I
Ratio Analysis as a Managerial Tool

Chapter 1 - Planning and Performance Management

Unfortunately, many company owners experience a rude awakening when their company, which a few years ago was doing well, suddenly finds itself facing tough competition and things start to go downhill. The cheque account has to be topped up constantly with extra loans, resulting in reduced freedom of action for the management. Eventually the company can be crushed by the increase in capital costs. There is no need to relate this story in greater detail, since most readers will know examples of strong companies that find themselves forced to close operations, after which they are either taken over by creditors or forced into liquidation.

Regrettably, there is no magic formula that managers can use to keep their companies profitable and competitive. The method proposed here is to introduce professional managerial practices and efficient means of budgeting and performance management. Managers are thus able to take a closer look at the economy of their company, and through analysis of possible future developments and trends, they are presented with early warnings and future scenarios.

Textbooks and journals on management are sometimes criticised for being too academic and off-putting for the business world. By its nature, the material covered in this chapter is academic and complex, but we will try to put it in plain language as far as possible. One way of doing this is to look at the subject from a new point of view- one that is familiar from another context. Consider, for example, how top athletes achieve results. Competition in athletics is as tough and ruthless as it is possible to imagine. Excuses are no good: only the best win.

Studies of high-achieving athletes show that those who go far have a future vision, a dream that drives them on. They may have their sights set on winning at the Olympic Games, being part of a national team or becoming the national champion. In general, athletes' dreams only come true if they follow plans: training- and competition schedules and plans of other types as appropriate. Taken together, such plans form an overall strategy.

If there is one special characteristic that sets top athletes apart from others, it is their setting of goals and assessment of results. Athletes must measure their progress. For example, their physical condition is assessed by means of lactic acid measurements, and athletes check constantly on whether their training is reflected in longer or higher jumps, longer throws, better track times, etc.

Sportsmen are quick to modify their plans and goals when unexpected events, such as injuries or lack of money, make it impossible for them to continue as they were. They keep a close eye on their rivals' successes and methods, since at the end of the day their own goals and standards have to take into account how others are doing.

When things go badly and they fail to achieve their goals, they take the appropriate measures. Such decisions are often painful, but have to be taken if success is to be achieved.

Many successful companies use methods similar to those used by top sportsmen. The terminology may differ, but the content is the same. Take, for example, measurements and the setting of goals. In the world of finance and strategic planning, this is called ratio analysis, while in Quality Management the term "bench-marking" is used.

In recent years, business schools, management consultants and business managers have given a great deal of attention to strategic planning. The books of management analysts have brought about a change of attitude on the part of many managers, and consultancy firms have been active promoting methods and assisting with strategic planning.

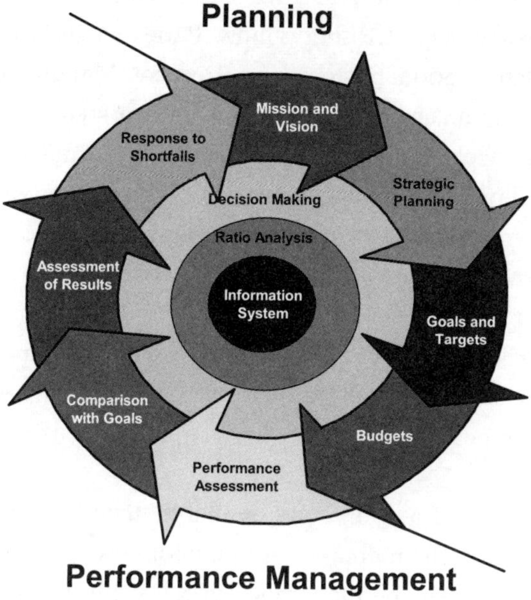

Fig. 1.1 - Model showing the interplay of planning and performance management.

Fig. 1.1 shows how planning and performance management are bound together in a continuous cycle, with planning and monitoring interlinked. The managers take decisions on the company's future (Strategic Planning), organise its activities (Operational Budgeting), tell the employees what the company is aiming at, and what standards and targets they set (Goals and Targets) and monitor the actual results (Performance Assessment and Comparison with Goals). But there is no point in stopping there: the results have to be assessed and if performance has fallen short of the goals, then appropriate measures must be taken. The experience gained is taken into account in drawing up the next set of plans and budgets, and so on.

Throughout this process, decisions are constantly being taken, whether formally or informally, consciously or unconsciously. How these decisions are taken will vary a great deal from one company to another.

The core of efficient planning and performance management is the information system. Fig. 1.1 shows how Ratio Analysis bridges the gap between the Information System and Decision-Making. Data from the Information System are packaged or transformed into simple and meaningful ratios relevant to decision making. Performance data is just as important in business management as it is in athletics. It places management control in a new context; through it, it is possible to connect budgeting and assessment to actual performance results.

Ratio Analysis can also be a powerful aid for competitive analysis. Companies can use it to compare their own operational results with those of their competitors.

If competitors' annual accounts are available, then their profitability and financial position can be mapped out in the same way as for the manager's own company. It has become much more common for companies to publish annual accounts or release information on their operational results in some other form. Even if not all the data are available, it is possible to estimate many of the figures that are lacking, or to obtain this information in other lawful ways. By monitoring the ratios of their main competitors from year to year, managers can put themselves in their position in order to understand their strengths and weaknesses and make forecasts about their ability to react to changed circumstances.

Just as it is possible to monitor individual companies, so it is useful to keep records of the operational outcome of the entire industry and to compare them with the performance of one's own company.

Before we go further in discussing the potential of financial indicators and ratios as tools in strategic business analysis, we shall give an overview of various commonly known and generally accepted financial ratios in the next chapter.

Chapter 2 - Financial Ratios

Financial ratios are produced from budgets and accounts in order to assess a company's performance and financial position. Ratio analysis is a quick method of gaining an insight into companies' strengths and weaknesses. Ratios are used all over the world as a sort of yardstick for assessing the results achieved. Therefore, managers should monitor trends in these ratios and make use of them when analysing their operations.

Financial ratios are usually analysed on an annualised basis, i.e., they are calculated from figures taken from the annual accounts. However, it is possible to calculate ratios for periods that are either shorter or longer than the normal accounting period. In such cases, care should be taken not to misinterpret the ratio. Let's take an example.

Inventory turnover during the first quarter of the operational period is 5.0 (i.e. sales amount to 5 times inventory during the quarter), average inventory amounts to $1,500,000 and sales for the quarter amount to $7,500,000.

If sales continue at the same level for the rest of the year, the year's sales will be $30,000,000. It is assumed that average inventory for the rest of the year will remain the same, $1,500,000. Therefore the annualised inventory turnover will be 20.0 (i.e. sales amount to 20 times inventory during the year).

We suggest that ratios of Income Statement and Balance Sheet figures, calculated for a period other than the normal accounting period, should also be expressed on an annualised basis.

This chapter falls into four sections dealing with the main types of ratios. Financial ratios are often grouped according to the type of information they give about the company's finances. The main types are:

- Profitability Ratios
- Activity Ratios
- Liquidity Ratios
- Leverage Ratios

2.1 Profitability Ratios

Return on Sales (ROS)

Indication: **Shows profit in relation to sales.**

Formula:

$$\frac{\text{Net profit after taxes}}{\text{Sales}}$$

Example:

- Net profit after taxes	700,000
- Sales	7,200,000

$$\frac{700{,}000}{7{,}200{,}000} = 9\%$$

Return on Sales, ROS, is a much-used ratio indicating the profitability of a company's operations, or how large a part of its operational revenues consists of net profit.

The ROS ratio says more than a profit figure in the Income Statement. Let us compare two companies.

A bank had a turnover of more than $11,000 million and declared a profit of $77.7 million. Its ROS was 0.007, or 0.7%. A computer company had a turnover of $1,000 million and a profit of $47 million. Its ROS was 0.047, or 4.7%.

The bank had a larger profit in $, but its turnover is ten times greater than that of the computer company. In terms of the scope of operations, the computer company achieved an operational result nearly seven times better than that of the bank.

Operating Profit Margin

Indication: **Shows profitability of basic operations.**

Formula:

$$\frac{\text{Earnings before interest \& taxes}}{\text{Sales}}$$

Example:

- Earnings after tax	1,095,000
- Interest	240,000
- Taxes	390,000
- Sales	7,200,000

$$\frac{1{,}095{,}000 + 240{,}000 + 390{,}000}{7{,}200{,}000} = 24\%$$

In order to neutralise the influence of a company's capital structure, it might be useful to ignore interest payments in the calculation of profit. A company whose finances are based largely on equity will have a higher ROS than one which is financed to a large extent by loan capital.

If data is available on a company's capital costs and tax payments, it can be useful to deduct these items from operating expenses (or add them to profit after tax) when calculating the Operating Profit Margin.

Companies may have deferred tax, the scope for making taxation adjustments varying from one company to another. This distorts the extent to which the ROS figures for different companies will be directly comparable. The same applies to the influence of company capital structure.

Return on Total Assets (ROA)

Indication: **Shows profit in relation to investments in assets.**

Formula:

$$\frac{\text{Net profit after taxes}}{\text{Total assets}}$$

Example:

- Net profit after taxes	700,000
- Total assets	10,960,000

$$\frac{700{,}000}{10{,}960{,}000} = 6\%$$

Naturally, it is expected that investments in a company should produce results in the form of improved operational performance. Money invested in production equipment, machines, computers, real estate and other assets should enhance competitiveness and generate profit. If this is not the case, then it is reasonable to consider larger dividends instead of investment within the company so that the owners can invest their money somewhere else where their capital can earn higher dividends.

On the other hand, owners must take care not to undermine the company's basis in the long term by withdrawing too much capital.

Return on Stockholders' Equity (ROE)

Indication: **Shows return on stockholders' investment.**

Formula:

$$\frac{\text{Net profit after taxes}}{\text{Total stockholders' equity}}$$

Example:

- Net profit after taxes	700,000
- Stockholders' equity	5,325,000

$$\frac{700{,}000}{5{,}325{,}000} = 13\%$$

The Return on Equity ratio, ROE, shows the profits which the owners make from the company's operations. It enables the owners to make a quick comparison between the profitability of their investment in the company and, e.g., interest rates offered by banks and other investment options.

In the accompanying computer models, it is possible to perform a "what-if" analysis of operational budgets and actual figures (see the DuPont Analysis discussed later). Through this, owners and managers can form an idea of on how well the company is doing with respect to Return on Equity.

Earnings per Share (EPS)

Indication: **Shows profit per common stock unit.**

Formula:

$$\frac{\text{Net profit after taxes}}{\text{Common stock}}$$

Example:

- Net profit after taxes	700,000
- Common stock	500,000

$$\frac{700{,}000}{500{,}000} = 140\%$$

Earnings per share (EPS) is similar to ROE in that it shows the owners' profits on the operations of the company. The difference is that instead of showing the profits on all the equity, it calculates the rate of profit on share capital only.

2.2 Activity Ratios

Inventory Turnover

Indication: **Shows capital tied up in inventories in terms of sales.**

Formula:

$$\frac{\text{Sales}}{\text{Average inventory}}$$

Example:

- Inventory 1/1	1,280,000
- Inventory 31/12	1,490,000
- Sales	7,200,000

$$\frac{7{,}200{,}000}{(1{,}280{,}000 + 1{,}490{,}000)/2} = 5.20$$

Most companies have to maintain inventories (stocks) to some extent. A trading company has stocks of items ready for sale, while a production company has raw material stocks, goods in the production process and stocks of final products. Inventories are more expensive than many managers realise. Generally, a great deal of capital is bound up in the inventories themselves, warehouses have to be built and staff have to be engaged to manage the stocks. Examples show that companies can achieve considerable rationalisation in their operations by restructuring their inventories and logistics.

A ratio which shows the inventory turnover, both as a percentage and in days, can therefore be extremely useful as a yardstick, for example in restructuring.

The most natural method is to calculate inventory turnover in terms of sales, i.e. sales / inventory. If this turnover figure is divided into 365, the average inventory collection in days is obtained, e.g. 365/5.2 = 70 days.

In the computer models, we have chosen to calculate average inventory within the quarter or year, as appropriate.

Accounts Receivable Turnover

Indication: **Shows capital tied up in accounts receivable in terms of sales.**

Formula:

$$\frac{\text{Sales}}{\text{Average accounts receivable}}$$

Example:

- Accounts receivable 1/1	1,150,000
- Accounts receivable 31/12	1,520,000
- Sales	7,200,000

$$\frac{7{,}200{,}000}{(1{,}150{,}000 + 1{,}520{,}000)/2} = 5.39$$

Company annual accounts may give a false impression of actual performance if they include accounts receivable which in fact might be lost, either partially or entirely. Moreover, receivables in the accounts automatically generate interest revenues which may possibly never be collected. Then, when the company faces the problem by means of write-offs, and even stopping dealing with particular debtors, operational losses may result. Thus, a growth in receivables may become a problem unless action is taken at the right time.

In the computer models we use the same methods to calculate ratios showing the Accounts Receivable Turnover as we used to calculate the Inventory Turnover.

Fixed Assets Turnover

Indication: **Reflects the extent to which plant, equipment and machinery are utilised.**

Formula:

$$\frac{\text{Sales}}{\text{Average fixed assets}}$$

Example:

- Fixed assets 1/1	2,060,000
- Fixed assets 31/12	2,025,000
- Sales	7,200,000

$$\frac{7{,}200{,}000}{(2{,}060{,}000 + 2{,}025{,}000)/2} = 3.53$$

Total Assets Turnover

Indication: **Shows utilisation of all the company's assets.**

Formula:

$$\frac{\text{Sales}}{\text{Average total assets}}$$

Example:

- Total assets 1/1	4,690,000
- Total assets 31/12	4,680,000
- Sales	7,200,000

$$\frac{7{,}200{,}000}{(4{,}690{,}000 + 4{,}680{,}000)/2} = 1.54$$

Ratios showing the Return on Fixed Assets and Return on Total Assets are intended to show how well the company's assets are being used to generate operational revenues.

These rates vary greatly between industries and sectors. Let us take a few examples:

Industry:	**Total Assets Turnover:**	**Fixed Assets Turnover:**
Dairy industry	1.2	1.9
Retail	1.9	5.6
Computer companies	1.9	4.7
Travel agencies, etc.	3.0	6.5

The turnover rates are lowest for the dairy industry and highest for travel agencies. This is explained by the fact that the dairy industry is characterised by a high level of investment, while travel agencies can operate without expensive production equipment.

In later chapters, and also in the computer models, we sometimes refer to the Total Assets Turnover ratio as Capital Efficiency (CE).

2.3 Liquidity Ratios

Current Ratio

Indication: **Shows the ability to meet short-term obligations.**

Formula:

$$\frac{\text{Current assets}}{\text{Current liabilities}}$$

Example:

- Current assets	2,965,000
- Current liabilities	1,640,000

$$\frac{2{,}965{,}000}{1{,}640{,}000} = 1.81$$

Quick Ratio

Indication: **Shows the ability to meet short-term obligations without needing to depend on sale of inventories.**

Formula:

$$\frac{\text{Current assets - Inventories}}{\text{Current liabilities}}$$

Example:

- Current assets	2,965,000
- Inventories	1,440,000
- Current liabilities	1,640,000

$$\frac{2{,}965{,}000 - 1{,}440{,}000}{1{,}640{,}000} = 0.93$$

Two ratios are generally used to assess a company's liquidity position: the Current Ratio and the Quick Ratio. The Current Ratio expresses the proportion of total current assets to current liabilities, while in the Quick Ratio the view is taken that inventories are in fact assets which can not easily be used to meet current liabilities. Thus it is said that current assets other than inventories are liquid current assets.

Long-term liquidity problems damage the company's performance, e.g. when it has to pay high interest on short-term loans, its creditworthiness is diminished and it is no longer able to embark on profitable investments.

Each individual company must decide for itself what Current Ratio and Quick Ratio figures are acceptable. This may depend on various factors, including the length of payment terms it has to grant its customers, the length of payment periods for its inventories and how quickly it pays off its long-term liabilities. Generally, however, it is considered that the Current Ratio should be at least 1.0.

2.4 Leverage Ratios

Equity Ratio (ER)

Indication: **Reveals the percentage of total funds supplied by shareholders.**

Formula:

$$\frac{\text{Shareholders' equity}}{\text{Total liabilities and shareholders' equity}}$$

Example:

- Shareholders' equity	3,325,000
- Total liabilities	7,345,000

$$\frac{3{,}325{,}000}{7{,}345{,}000 + 3{,}325{,}000} = 31\%$$

The Equity Ratio, ER, indicates the proportion of equity to the company's total capital. Then the proportion of liabilities is also a known quantity (e.g. if the Equity Ratio is 40%, then the proportion of liabilities is 60%).

The Equity Ratio indicates how well prepared the company is to deal with setbacks, additional capital costs and losses. A company with a low Equity Ratio does not have what is known as "patient capital". This means that it might lack room for manoeuvre, e.g. if it wants to move into new markets or embark on expensive product development.

A company with a low Equity Ratio is in a weak position if its competitors lower their prices or attack it in some other way through the market.

The Equity Ratio is the focal point of this book and is discussed in more detail in the following chapters.

Book Value per Common Stock

Indication: **Reveals the value of common stock according to the balance sheet. Not necessarily the market value.**

Formula:

$$\frac{\text{Shareholders' equity}}{\text{Common stock}}$$

Example:

- Shareholders' equity	3,325,000
- Common stock	745,000

$$\frac{3{,}325{,}000}{745{,}000} = 4.46$$

Book Value per Common Stock shows the value of common stock according to the accounts. It is the ratio: Shareholders' Equity/Common Stock.

A high Book Value of shareholders' equity reflects profitable operations, since the profits of the past few years have added to the company's equity. In the same way, loss erodes equity. If the Book Value of shareholders' equity is lower than 1.0 then the owners have lost part of the capital they invested in the company.

The Book Value per Common Stock is not the market value of the shares. Investors might find the company so attractive that they will be prepared to pay a premium for its shares. This happens when a company buys out a competitor company in order to increase its market share, reduce the number of competitors and pool investments in the interests of rationalisation. On the other hand, the market price of shares may be lower than the book value, for example in the case of a company facing unfavourable external circumstances.

We shall discuss the concept of "economic goals" in modern business management in the next chapter. As we shall see, the Equity Ratio should be a key economic goal. Strategic budgeting, which is discussed in Chapter 4, must therefore focus on the development of the Equity Ratio.

Chapter 3 – The Equity Ratio

3.1 Using the Equity Ratio instead of Profit as the Key Objective in Strategic Management

Management of change and strategic management in modern business, requires an expanded view upon the concept of economies and the system of control. The goal of established economic theory - maximum profit - and the means of controlling it were created for enterprises that had to cope with a simpler and far less dynamic world than the present one. They therefore cannot be considered satisfactory for management that has to cope with a multiple concept of goals and rapidly changing conditions.

For many stakeholders, such as shareholders, external sources of finance and boards of directors and managers, the size of profit is still the basis for assessment of the quality of a company. Most stakeholders are happy if the profit achieved is bigger than last year or bigger than budgeted, no matter the amount of resources that was needed in order to achieve this profit, and no matter the effect on the company's ability to survive.

What really matters is whether the actual profit is sufficient for financing a reasonable part of future investments needed for expansion and new development. In order to secure long-range survival, the company must balance its profit and changes in assets to enable it to maintain a reasonable ratio of equity capital. A company that wants to survive in a dynamic world must comply with criteria other than the mere difference between income and costs. In a business in which a considerable part of the financial resources is provided by external sources, it will be an absolute requirement to take the following into account:

- banks' and other stakeholders' need for security (collateral)
- employees' desire for long-term employment
- customers' need for continuity

- society's requirements regarding employment
- suppliers' need for collateral.

A way of meeting all these requirements would be to maintain an equity ratio that is acceptable for these stakeholders and secures the company's long-range survival. If the company fails to fulfil such requirements, this will result in loss of freedom of action for the management, a reduction of the company's scope for engaging in development activities and an inability to exploit emerging opportunities. The model "ER-Prop", described in Section 7.1.1, calculates proposals for the Equity Ratio based on the strategic position of the company.

Ensuring that the company preserves the necessary ratio of equity capital during expansion and development involves focusing on the balance between profit, growth rate and asset growth. The evaluation of a company and the quality of managerial decisions must therefore be based on its ability to finance future investments through maintenance of a reasonable Equity Ratio.

The desired Equity Ratio can be achieved through a stock issue or by seeking other forms of venture capital, but a great many companies are forced to build up their equity capital by making profit. However, an Equity Ratio is not created solely by making profit, but by balancing profit, growth and changes in assets. Profitability is not merely a question of the difference between income and costs, but rather the ability to approach a targeted Equity Ratio, while a drift away from the targeted ratio should be regarded as a problem.

Making the Equity Ratio the economic objective makes sense because a low Equity Ratio often creates a cash flow shortage and loss of freedom of action. It also prevents the company from engaging in development programs without the support of external financial sources, even if such programs are considered vital for its survival. At the same time, a low

Equity Ratio reduces the confidence of banks, suppliers and other external financial sources. A low Equity Ratio also reduces the management's willingness to take calculated risks and thus prevents the company from seizing emerging opportunities.

Maintaining a high Equity Ratio, on the other hand, reduces the company's ability to compete because it may force it to operate with a higher profit rate, smaller investments or lower growth rate than its competitors. Therefore, both a policy of maintaining a high Equity Ratio and a policy of keeping a low Equity Ratio will reduce the company's ability to engage in development or take risks. Strategic management must maintain or establish an Equity Ratio that is high enough to:

- provide the necessary freedom of action
- secure the ability to adapt to changes in the environment or customer behaviour
- secure the ability to engage in necessary or desired development
- secure the confidence of shareholders, banks, suppliers and other stakeholders

yet not so high that it reduces the company's ability to compete.

3.2 *Managing the Equity Ratio*

Making the Equity Ratio (ER) the key objective of management planning and control would not be meaningful unless it were possible to control the way it will develop.

The formula below calculates the limit of the Equity Ratio, ER_n, which is the value that the present actual ER will converge towards. With the formulas and models provided by this book, we are able to predict how the ER will develop, e.g. over the next 5 or 10 years. The model ER-Value, which is described in Section 7.1.2. , has been designed for this purpose.

The three elements of the Equity Ratio are:

- Net Profit Rate (NPR) $= \frac{\text{Profit after Taxes - Dividend}}{\text{Sales}}$
- Capital Efficiency, CE (earlier referred to as Total Assets Turnover, see Section 2.2),
- Growth rate, G.

Since we are focusing on equity and the Equity Ratio, we define NPR as the profit that remains in the company, or the means of increasing the equity and thus financing the expansion of assets.

According to the formula, the Equity Ratio will tend towards a value, ER_n, which will depend entirely on the average return on sales, the average growth rate and the capital efficiency at a given time.

$$ER_n \longrightarrow \frac{NPR * CE_n}{G}$$

This model predicts the financial status of a company if operations carry on as usual or according to strategic budgets. A budget is a yardstick for controlling short-term activities. Correspondingly, the ER_n is an indication as to whether the plans and chosen strategies will lead to the desired financial position. If the actual ER_n diverges in any way from the ER_{goal}, this will require changes in plans and strategies. During any forecasting period, events will occur that will change, or even invalidate chosen strategies, which means that changes in ER_n require constant surveillance and, if need be, corrective action.

The formula establishes the long-range ER and is in fact independent of its present level. This development is shown in the graph below. We see that both curves converge towards the same limit. One curve starts at 0.5 and tends towards the limit (ER_n), falling below 0.3 after more than 20 periods/years. The second curve starts at 0.1 and tends towards the same limit as the first. The essence is that both are produced by the same NPR, CE and G.

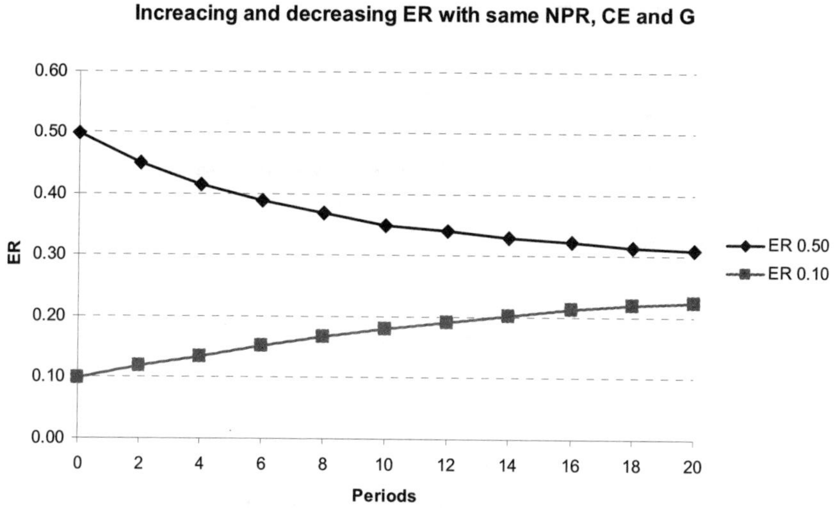

Fig. 3.1 – The long-range ER is independent of its present level.

A given combination of NPR, CE and G will always create the same end-value. The greater G is, the greater the speed at which the ER will approach its limit.

As is shown in the curves below, a negative ER trend may be slow if the growth rate G is small, and consequently it will take several periods before the ER will reach a critical value. If the growth rate is high, the ER will reach the critical value faster, which will call for immediate corrective action. Early corrective action will have a greater impact than action taken after an unsatisfactory ER value has been reached.

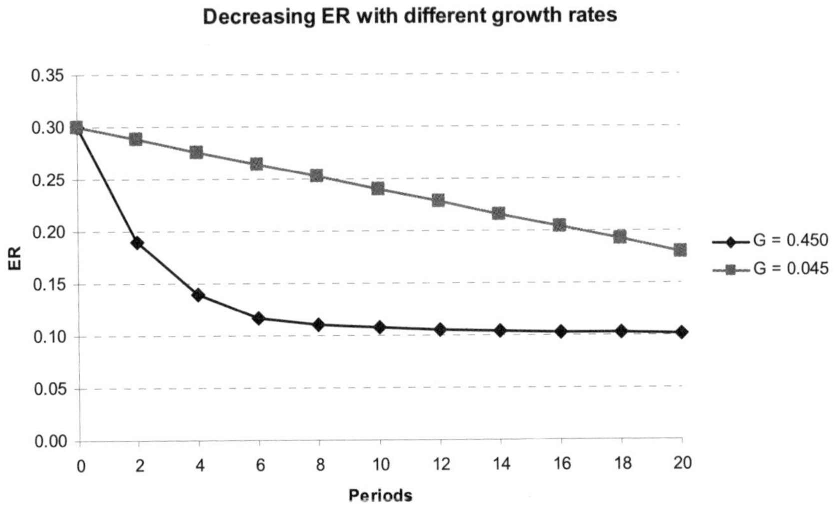

Fig. 3.2 - Decreasing ER with different Growth rates.

A trend towards an unsatisfactory Equity Ratio can be corrected by increasing the net return on sales (NPR), raising the capital efficiency (CE) or reducing the growth rate (G).

Most companies sell a number of different products or product lines, and in most cases to different customers. Different products will normally create different returns on sales and require different levels of investments. Likewise, sales made to different customers or groups of customers may result in different rates of return on sales: the customers may require different discounts, different product variations or product adaptations, or demand different terms of payment. This means that the company will have scope to improve its ER by expanding on product and/or customer segments with the highest NPR and/or CE. A special model, Product and Market Portfolio, which is described in Section 7.3.1, has been designed for analysis of expansion scenarios.

The problem is that products with high net return and high capital efficiency are sometimes combined with customers or customer groups in combinations that yield low net return and low capital efficiency. Therefore it is necessary to identify combinations of products/customers with high net return and high capital efficiency:

		Capital Efficiency, CE	
		LOW	**HIGH**
Net Profit Rate, NPR	**HIGH**	B: product/customer segment, where profit ratio should be improved before expansion is planned	A: product/customer segment, where expansion can take place at high profit and small investments: Expansion base
	LOW	D: product/customer segment, where both profit and capital efficiency must be improved before expansion if any at all is planned	C: product/customer segment, where capital efficiency should be improved before expansion is planned

Figure 3.3 - Product / Customer combination

The way the Equity Ratio develops determines the management's future freedom of action and the company's ability to adapt to changes. Thus, the current ER and the direction in which it is evolving is a tool for evaluating:

- appropriate actions for initiating a turn-around process
- the company's actual and future financial strength, and consequently its ability to survive
- the company's present and future capacity to initiate the adjustments called for by changes in the environment or chosen goals
- the quality of a chosen strategy
- the skill and quality of the management
- the value of the company in connection with a merger or take-over.

In other words, the evolution of the ER is a parameter that must be taken into consideration in planning the company's strategies and future development. The model, "ER-Pos", which is described in Section 7.1.3, graphically illustrates the strategic situation of the company based on the Equity Ratio. Each position is provided with an evaluation and a general recommendation for future directions.

Chapter 4 – Strategic Budgeting

4.1 *Ratio Analysis of Short-Term Traditional Budgets*

It is vital that managers should avoid getting bogged down in petty details and not seeing the wood for the trees when drawing up operational budgets. The computer models accompanying this book are aids for examining operational budgets to see whether they will deliver sufficient profitability, i.e. whether they will reduce the company's solvency, whether assets contribute sufficiently to the creation of revenues, etc. Financial ratios calculated in this way then become operational targets.

Ratio analysis can thus be applied as a managerial tool for implementing strategic thinking in the process of preparing annual budgets.

In principle, two methods of ratio analysis can be used in operational budgeting:

1. The "top-down" method, in which budgeting begins with ratio analysis.
2. The "bottom-up" method, in which a draft operational budget is prepared in the normal way, after which ratio analysis is performed to see whether the draft will produce acceptable results.

The "Top-Down" Method

Managers begin preparing their budget by making assumptions about revenues and expenses. They assume certain figures for the year as a whole and then divide them to produce figures for each quarter or month. Initially, this division may be a matter of simple proportions. To use the accompanying computer models, the figures are entered in the first worksheet in the model.

If the balance-sheet total is not available at the beginning of the year when the budget is drawn up, then the financial items will have to be estimated on the basis of available data.

When the estimated revenues and expenses for each year have been entered, and also the financial position at the beginning of the operational period, the model will calculate the financial ratios for the budget. The managers can then assess whether the aim expressed in their budget will produce sufficient profitability. Ratio analysis can also reveal excessive optimism in the assumptions. It is easy to change the assumptions and examine the consequences, i.e. to perform a "what-if" analysis.

When the managers are satisfied with the outcome, the key premises for the operational budget have been established. The target for the following year's operations has been defined, and also a cost framework that is considered realistic.

The next step in preparing the budget is to apply it to individual departments and operational units.

The "Bottom-Up" Method

Preparation of the budget begins with departmental managers drawing up a draft budget for their departments or operational units. Such drafts ought to be based on an analysis of competition and strategic planning, though previous budgets and outcome figures are also taken into consideration up to a point. When this is done, the departmental budgets are combined in a draft overall budget. The managers take the figures resulting from this budget and enter them into the computer model. The outcome is examined and considered in terms of profitability and other targets as discussed above. Changes are then made, as appropriate, and when the managers are satisfied with the outcome, the earlier drafts are modified accordingly.

In the data entry sheet in the computer models, it is expected that outcome figures for each month or quarter will be entered for comparison with the budget. It is vital to check on whether budgets are realised, and to take measures if this is not the case. In this way it is easy for managers to introduce efficient performance management.

Entering a draft of an operational budget in the DuPont Model (a separate worksheet in the computer models) demonstrates graphically how certain ratios are formed on the basis of capital at the beginning of the operational period and of operational financial performance.

If new values are entered for revenues and expenses and/or the asset situation, the model will calculate the ratios anew. Thus, the DuPont Model can be used as an analytical tool (what-if analysis) for decision making and the setting of goals.

4.2 *Implementing Long-Term Strategic Budgets*

As mentioned in Chapter 3, the Equity Ratio, and especially its long-term development, can be considered a yardstick of the company's ability to survive.

However, the goal for the Equity Ratio cannot be set objectively. Neither can an appropriate Equity Ratio be a fixed and unchangeable quantity. It must be tailored to the specific company and the conditions under which it operates. A number of factors have to be taken into consideration and weighted individually for each company, for instance:

- Standards and risks of the trade. The higher the risk, the higher the Equity Ratio that will be required.
- The average Equity Ratio of the industry and trade. Expectations of banks and other external financial resources vary from society to society.
- Frequency and scope of changes in the environment. The more frequent and drastic changes, the higher the Equity Ratio that will be needed.

- Dependency on specific customers. Dependency on a few important customers involves a higher risk and requires a higher Equity Ratio.
- Anticipation of future competition. The more vigorous the future competition is expected to be, the higher the Equity Ratio that will be required.
- Investments deriving from expansion. The lower such investments are, the lower the Equity Ratio that can be accepted.

Such factors will be specific for each enterprise and must be evaluated individually. Though they are qualitative factors, they can be evaluated quantitatively and thus help to establish a goal for the company's Equity Ratio. But when quantified, the calculated goal can only be a guideline for the stipulation of the goal. Management's judgement and experience gives a differentiated picture of what ratio is necessary, and why.

Chapter 8 describes the computer model that accompanies this book and is designed for creating and analysing strategic budgets. The chapter explains how to use the model and discusses various examples. Figure 4.1 below is a printout from the model.

As can be seen from Figure 4.1, there are three Equity Ratio values: the ER-budget, the ER-limit and the ER-goal.

Company: **Company X Ltd.**

Amounts in: **GBP**

Strategic budget:

	Year 0	Year 1				Year 2				Year 3			
	Results Y0	Cap. Eff.	NPR	Growth rate	**Results Y1**	Cap. Eff.	NPR	Growth rate	**Results Y2**	Cap. Eff.	NFR	Growth rate	**Results Y3**
Key Figures:													
Annual Sales	**1,515**	**1.080**	**0.024**	**0.055**	1,598	**1.050**	**0.022**	**0.075**	1,718	**1.100**	**0.020**	**0.089**	1,871
Net profit					38				38				37
Equity	**411**				449				487				525
Total Assets	**1,263**				1,480				1,636				1,701
Equity Ratios:													
Equity Ratio - Budget	0.326				0.304				0.298				0.308
Equity Ratio - Limit	**0.330**				0.471				0.308				0.247
Equity Ratio - Goal					**0.350**				**0.360**				**0.370**

Figure 4.1 – A model for creating and analysing strategic budgets.

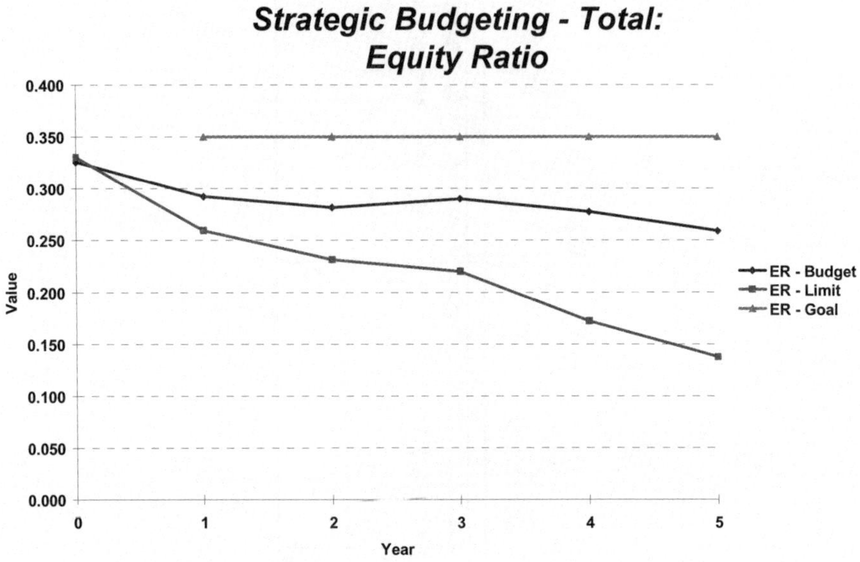

Figure 4.2 – A graphical presentation of ER-budget, ER-Limit and ER-goal.

The ER-goal is the Equity Ratio that is considered to be appropriate for the company. In this example the ER-goal, 0.35, is fixed for the entire period, but it could be a different value for each year. The model "ER-Prop" is a tool for analysing the appropriate ER-goal for a company.

The ER-budget value is the calculation of the actual Equity Ratio for each year based on the assumptions in the budget. It is obtained by dividing total equity by total assets.

The ER-limit is the value discussed in the previous chapter, and is given by the formula:

$$ER_n \longrightarrow \frac{NPR * CE_n}{G}$$

The ER-Limit is the value which the Equity Ratio converges towards. This means that the Equity Ratio will eventually become that value if the situation stays unchanged for a sufficient length of time. As can be seen from Figure 4.1, the ER-limit changes from one period to the next according to changes in the assumptions of the formula.

Strategic budgeting requires assessment of some key operating and balance-sheet figures, such as sales, costs and profit after tax, dividends, etc., during, e.g., a five-year period. Assumptions of future capital efficiency, growth rate and net profit rate are based on these figures. These three assumptions are the only parameters necessary for applying the model.

For net profit rate (NPR) in the simulations, one can use last year's NPR, an average of the past few years' NPR, a forecast NPR calculated as the correlation of the past few years' NPR or even an arbitrary value.

The capital efficiency (CE) shows the amount of sales the company has been able to achieve historically by its investments in assets; e.g. a capital efficiency of 1.1 shows that the company has been able to create sales of $1.1 per dollar invested. The higher the capital efficiency, the more efficiently the company has been able to utilise its investments.

Analysis of Scandinavian statistics shows that both short-term and long-term capital efficiency for the economy as a whole is remarkably constant, and is not influenced either shortage of capital or fluctuations in interest rates. Even analysis of many companies' balance sheets shows that they operate with constant capital efficiency even if there are fluctuations in operating results from year to year, which could mean that capital efficiency is a neglected managerial tool.

Increasing capital efficiency means cutting assets at the existing sales level or expanding sales at a given investment level. An increase in capital efficiency can be considered a tool for achieving a desired Equity Ratio.

However, it must be taken into consideration that decreasing assets compared to sales in many situations will have a strategic impact, which again means that such decisions should be made in connection with strategic planning and should always be part of the planning process. Assets are normally divided into two groups: current and fixed assets. For strategic purposes, it might be worthwhile to analyse assets from a different angle, namely as:

- policy-derived assets
- supplier-derived assets
- customer-derived assets.

Policy-derived assets are assets that are rendered necessary by the company's own choice of policy or systems, e.g. choice of domicile, choice of technology, choice of delivery policy or credit policy.

Supplier-derived assets are assets resulting from the supplier's choice of policy, e.g. delivery policy.

Customer-derived assets are assets linked to the choice of customers or customer segments and marketing efforts, e.g. customers buying only customer-designed products or customers buying standard products, customers requiring special terms of payment, etc.

As has been mentioned already, changes in these or other factors will often have a strategic impact, but equally often, a close analysis reveals assets that are not absolutely necessary and can be reduced or even disposed of without any strategic or practical impact.

In simulations, the capital efficiency (CE) value can be stated as last year's figure, an average over a period, a correlated value or an arbitrarily chosen value.

The growth rate (G) is the annual increase in sales volume. In simulations, last year's growth rate, an average over a period, a correlated value or an arbitrarily chosen value can be used.

Part II

User's Guide to the Computer Models

Chapter 5 – Introduction

Part I of this book discussed the use of ratio analysis as a managerial tool. It examined the use of financial indicators and ratios in e.g. preparing budgets, both operational and strategic, and pointed out various other purposes for which they can be used, including performance management, competition analysis and prediction of the future development of the Equity Ratio.

Part II is devoted to the computer models on the accompanying CD, with a description of the models and their use.

As is stated in the Introduction, the models calculate financial indicators based on the company's past financial performance and different future scenarios. They should serve the needs of most companies, regardless of their size and line of business.

The models are designed with the intention of making data entry as simple as possible. Only a few figures need to be entered in order to obtain financial indicators and a graphic presentation of the data. The models are based on "live" data entry, i.e. indicators and graphs are revised each time new values are entered.

5.1 Getting started

One CD disc accompanies this book. It is divided into two parts. One part contains the basic data files which can be used to create working models for all companies. The other part contains demonstration examples.

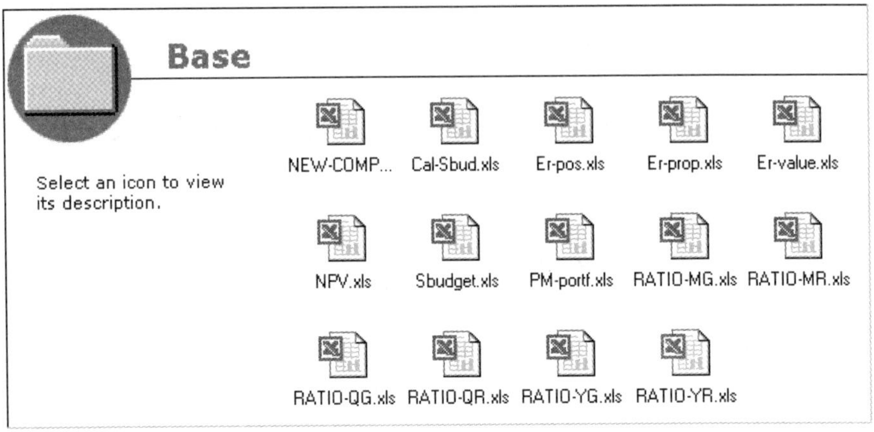

Fig. 5.1 – The basic data files for the models.

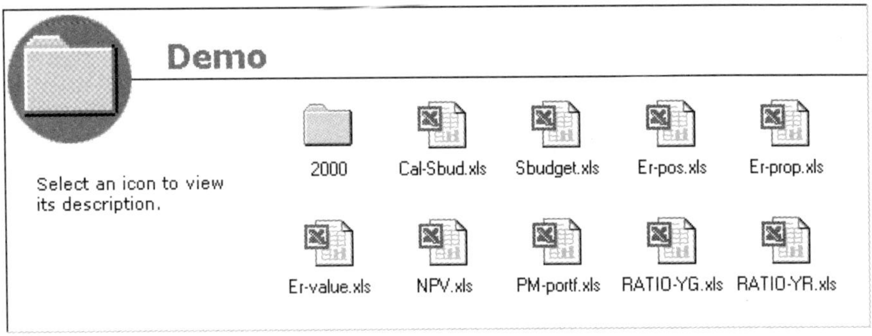

Fig. 5.2 – The demonstration data files for the models.

The discussion of the models in the following chapters is divided into Operational Ratio Analysis and Strategic Ratio Analysis. Models for Operational Ratio Analysis are described in Section 5.2 and further in Chapter 6. Models for Strategic Ratio Analysis are described in Section 5.3 and further in Chapter 7.

5.2 Models for Operational Ratio Analysis

5.2.1 Main documents – Ratio and Graph documents

The model for Operational Ratio Analysis consists of 6 documents:

1. **RATIO-YR.XLS** - Ratio analysis showing developments from one year to the next.
2. **RATIO-YG.XLS** - Graphic presentation of the data from the data document RATIO-YR.XLS.

3. **RATIO-QR.XLS** - Ratio analysis for each operational year, by quarters.
4. **RATIO-QG.XLS** - Graphic presentation of the data from the data document RATIO-QR.XLS.

5. **RATIO-MR.XLS** - Ratio analysis for each operational year, by months.
6. **RATIO-MG.XLS** - Graphic presentation of the data from the data document RATIO-MR.XLS.

Documents 1 and 2 (RATIO-YR and RATIO-YG) function together as an independent unit; the same applies to documents 3 and 4 (quarters) and documents 5 and 6 (months). See Fig. 5.3.

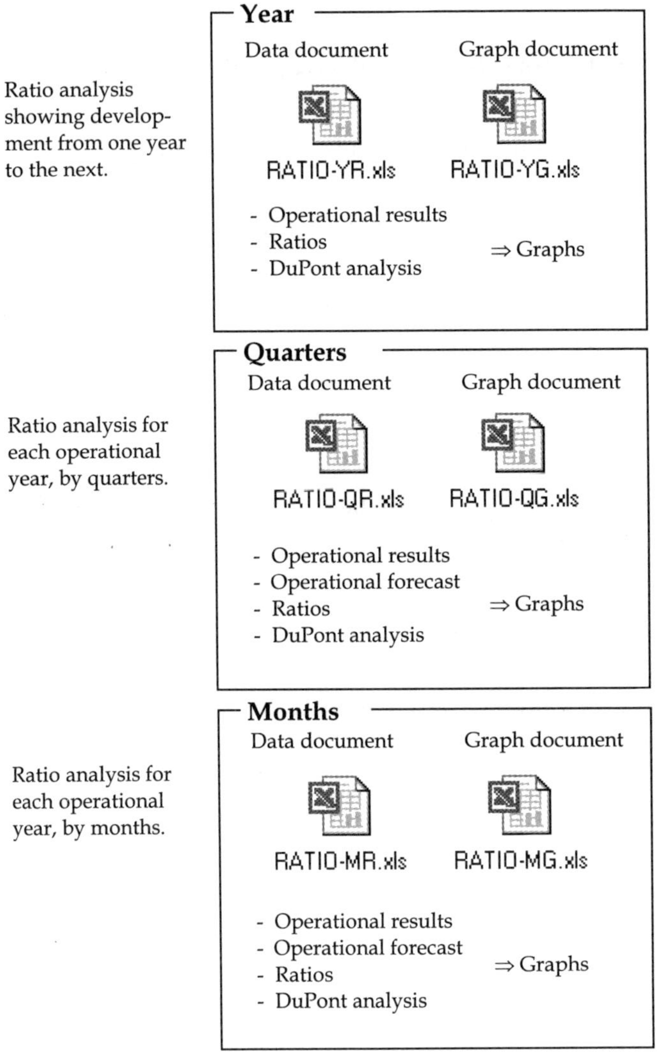

Fig. 5.3 - How the base documents function together. All changes made in a data document are automatically transferred to the document handling graphic presentation.

Data documents and graph documents for companies and years are linked when they are created. The link between the documents is expressed as follows:

Data documents: The company name will appear at the top of the "Statements" worksheet.

Graph documents: The company name will appear at the top of the "Graph Data" worksheet.

The user can decide whether or not he wants to use all three parts of the model. Some users may, e.g., wish to use only the part of the model which shows changes from one year to the next, together with a quarterly analysis of each year.

5.2.2 Entering data

Worksheets (see Fig. 5.4) make it possible to browse in a sort of card index in the model. The user is able to move to a new sheet by simply pressing on the tab. All data are entered into one worksheet, "Statements". Other worksheets show the calculated results.

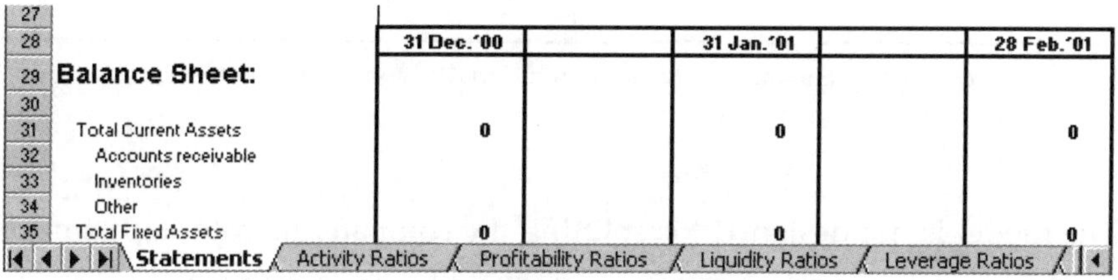

Fig. 5.4 – All data is entered into the "Statements" worksheet.

NB: THE NAMES OF TABS MAY NOT BE CHANGED

If a tab's name is changed, some of the programs in the model will not work properly.

To ensure the reliable functioning of the model, a large part of it has been protected so as to make changes impossible. The only parts which are not protected are the data entry areas and the title areas which the user may want to change.

The "Statements" worksheet is structured as follows.

Income Statement:

Net Sales:

Costs and Expenses:
- (free text)
- (free text)
- (free text)
- (free text)
- (free text)

Depreciation
Interest expense
Taxes

Net Income:

Balance Sheet:

Total Current Assets
Accounts receivable
Inventories
- (free text)

Total Fixed Assets
- (free text)
- (free text)
- (free text)

Total Assets:

Total Current Liabilities
Total Long-Term Debt

Total Liabilities:

Shareholders' Equity
Common Stock
- (free text)

Total Liabilities and Shareholders' Equity:

Fig. 5.5 - Income statement and balance sheet items in the model's data entry worksheet.

The model is not designed for splitting the company up into departments, product-lines or profit-centres. To be able to examine indicators for individual departments, product-lines or profit-centres, a special document must be created for each such operational unit. In such cases, costs and expenses and balance sheet figures must be itemised accordingly.

The minimum itemisation of Costs and Expenses consists of four lines:

- Operational costs and expenses
- Depreciation
- Interest expense
- Taxes.

Operational costs and expenses can then be itemised further (maximum 5 lines). The base documents in the model use the following itemisation:

- Direct production costs
- Other production costs
- Sales
- Research and development
- General and administrative costs.

To change names, overwrite the existing text. If fewer lines are required, the others must be left blank.

The model's itemisation of Current Assets is fixed as follows:

- Accounts receivable
- Inventories
- Other.

The name "Other" can be changed. Inventories and Accounts Receivable must be entered in order to be able to calculate the Inventories and Accounts Receivable turnover ratios.

It is not essential to itemise Fixed Assets, since they only appear as an aggregate item in the model's indicators. The following itemisation is used in the model's base documents:

- Properties
- Equipment
- Other.

In User ratios (see Appendix B) it may be interesting to calculate, e.g. "Property turnover" or "Equipment turnover" (instead of Fixed Assets Turnover as a whole, as is calculated in the model's standard ratios.)

Short-term liabilities are combined in a single figure.

Long-term liabilities are not used for the calculation of standard ratios, but form a basis for total liabilities, and are therefore necessary.

Equity is to be divided into:

- Stockholders' Equity
- Other Equity.

It is essential to specify Stockholders' Equity separately so as to be able to calculate both Return on Shares and the Book Value of Shares If no data on this division is available, then the item "Other Equity" may be changed to Total Equity and Equity can be entered there as a single figure. In that case, Book Value per Common Stock and Earnings per Share will not be calculated, but other ratios based on equity will be calculated.

5.2.3 Ratios and DuPont Analysis

As has already been stated, all indicators in the system are calculated automatically as soon as new data is entered. Explanations of the indicators are to be found in Sections 6.1 and 6.2; an introduction to using DuPont Analysis is to be found in Section 6.3.

The user may create his own indicators and make them into standard information in the model. User indicators are explained in Appendix B.

5.2.4 Graphical presentation

15 standard graphs have been set up for graphic presentation of Income Statement and Balance Sheet items and indicators.

The user may create his own graphs and make them into standard graphs in the model. See Appendix B for further details.

5.3 Models for Strategic Ratio Analysis

5.3.1 Main documents

The models consists of six main documents and one support document:
The main documents are:

1. **ER-PROP.XLS** - A model for identifying the appropriate (required) Equity Ratio, based on analysis of the strategic position of the company.

2. **ER-VALUE.XLS** - Models to calculate the future development of the Equity Ratio.

3. **ER-POS.XLS** - A matrix for identifying the company's actual strategic situation in the context of the Equity Ratio. The model includes recommendations / evaluation of the situation.

4. **SBUDGET.XLS** - Models for strategic budgeting.

5. **PM-PORTF.XLS** - A model for analysing potential future market / product portfolio scenarios.

6. **NPV.XLS** – Models to calculate the value of a company based on the equity surplus when the Equity Ratio is fixed over a period of 5, 7 or 10 years.

   The support document is:

7. **CAL-SBUD.XLS** – A tool for calculating:
   a) The Capital Efficiency based on Liquidity, Return on Investments and the profit margin **(U-values)**.
   b) Trends in Net Profit Rate and Growth, based on historical data **(Correlation Calc)**.

5.3.2 The Overall Functionality

Each document is an independent unit. They are linked together, so they can either be used for specific analysis of isolated issues or to produce a broad overview of the strategic position / future development of a company.

Some of the documents include a number of worksheets. Some of the worksheets are for data analysis and some are for graphical presentation of the results.

ER-PROP.XLS is a document that enables the user to calculate a proposal for the ER goal. The documents contains a number of elements that should be considered and weighted for the purpose of setting an appropriate ER goal. It must be understood that the program does not pretend to set an objective ER goal but only to make a proposal that the management can use in its subjective goal setting.

NPV.XLS calculates the value of the company at the present time, leaving it to the owners to consider whether it would be worth while carrying on present operations in the expectation of future profit or whether it would be a better idea to try to sell the company immediately.

ER-VALUE.XLS calculates future values of the ER, based on the assumption that operations will continue on their present lines without any alterations being made, and at the same time indicating whether major changes in strategy or business concept are advisable.

ER-POS.XLS shows the present or future position of the ER compared to the ER goal and gives an evaluation of the chosen strategy, at the same time giving recommendations on improved strategy if needed.

SBUDGET.XLS is a framework for strategic budgeting, which means focusing on the Equity Ratio and integrating it with growth in sales and changes in assets. This linking is often neglected in normal planning because of the common belief that expansion will automatically lead to increased profit and better utilisation of investments that have already been made. In fact, growth *per se* seldom means either larger profits or higher capital efficiency.

The structure of strategic budgeting therefore derives from a set goal for future Equity Ratio and involves adjusting net profit, capital efficiency and the growth rate until a satisfactory result is achieved.

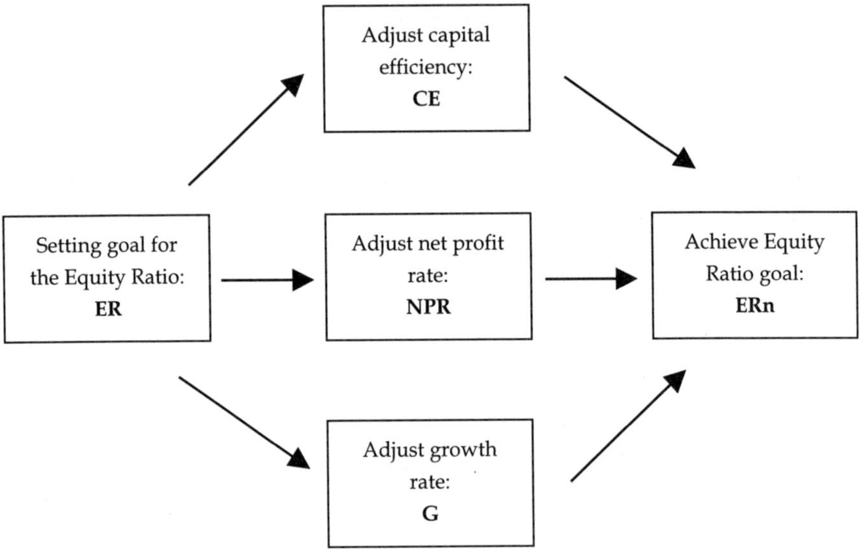

Fig. 5.6 – The structure of Strategic Budgeting.

The basic idea of strategic budgeting is that achieving the set Equity Ratio goal is essential for the company's survival, and that all activities must be subordinated to this goal. This in turn means that any expansion must take the evolution of the Equity Ratio into consideration. If the goal cannot be achieved, adjustments must be carried out either by:

- Increasing the net profit rate, or
- Increasing the capital efficiency, or
- Decreasing the growth rate (the expansion rate), or
- A combined adjustment of all three elements, or
- Choosing a specific expansion bases that will make it possible to achieve the Equity Ratio goal.

All models in the Strategic Budgeting program are designed either to set the Equity Ratio goal or to evaluate whether the goal is being achieved or will be achieved through on-going operations, or to enable the company to identify measures that must be taken in order to achieve the goal. Furthermore, the model enables the user to draw up budgets based on a different net profit rate, capital efficiency and growth rate for different combinations of products / customers or product groups / customer groups.

PM-PORTF.XLS is designed to rank product/customers or product-groups/customers-groups in order to select groups with a high net profit rate and high capital efficiency or neglect groups with a low net profit rate and low capital efficiency.

CAL-SBUD.XLS can be used as an aid for setting the values of the Growth rate, Net Profit Rate and Capital Efficiency in any of the above-mentioned models.

Chapter 6 Using the Models for Operational Ratio Analysis

6.1 Annual Ratio Analysis by quarters or months

As has been stated above, it is possible to work with the results (or forecasts) of each operational year by months and/or quarters. Monthly or quarterly analysis is essentially the same. In order to avoid repetition, all explanations are based on quarterly ratio analysis.

The main difference between monthly and quarterly analysis is as follows:

Quarterly analysis:	**Monthly analysis:**
The model is divided into quarters.	The model is divided into the 12 months of the year.
The closing figures for the quarters are then added together in 6-, 9- and 12-monthly total columns.	There is no total column. Each month is independent.
Data document: RATIO-QR.XLS Graph document: RATIO-QG.XLS	Data document: RATIO-MR.XLS Graph document: RATIO-MG.XLS

6.1.1 Creating new years

Worksheets for new years for each company are created in one of the already existing QR (quarterly) or MR (monthly) worksheets. It is not possible to create a new year from a YR (annual) worksheet.

Select "New year" from the "Models" menu.

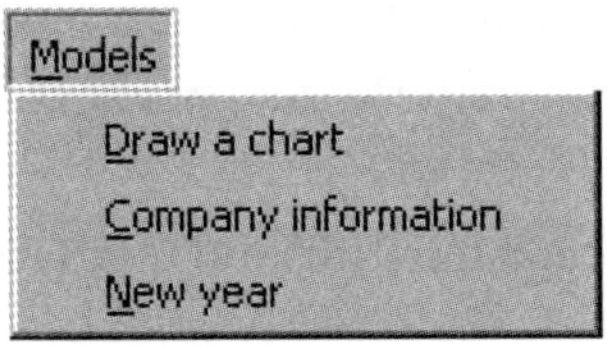

Fig. 6.1 - The "Models" menu.

This displays the menu for creating new years. Enter the year in "New year" and confirm your choice with "New year". The model will then create a new folder and working documents for the new year. The folder will be marked with the year.

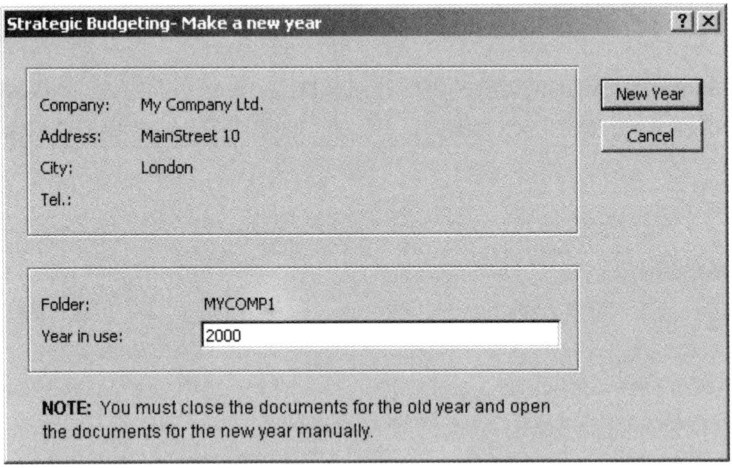

Fig. 6.2 - Menu for creating new years.

The model does not automatically open the new document when a new year is created. To open a working document for a new year, the corresponding working document for the previous year must first be closed.
Fig. 6.3 shows the folder structure for working documents for each year for each company.

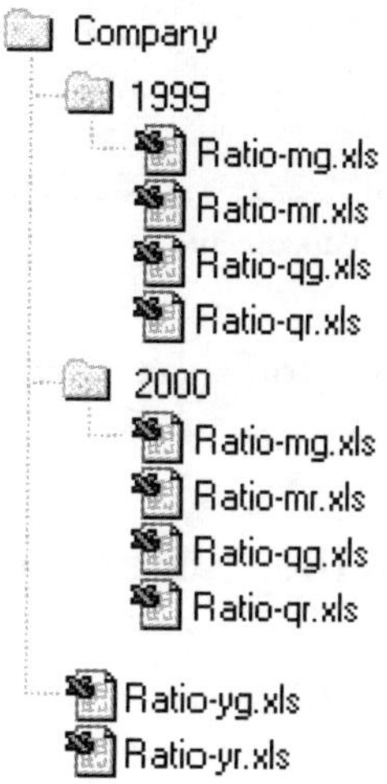

Fig. 6.3 - Folder structure showing a company's working documents for each year.

It will be noticed that the working documents in all the files have the same names. Thus, the distinction between them can only be seen from their position in the folder structure. The properties of a document can be seen in two ways:

a) Select "Information" from the "Model" menu.

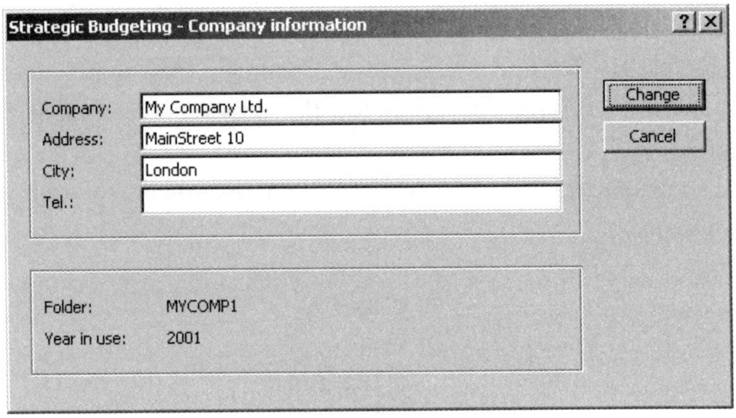

Fig. 6.4 - Properties and data about a document.

b) Select the "Statements" worksheet. Details of the company and year appear at the top of the sheet.

6.1.2 Entry of data in the "Statements" worksheet

Basic document: **RATIO-QR.XLS**
Worksheet: **Statements**

Changes made to the column headings in the "Statements" worksheet will appear elsewhere in the model. Therefore it is sufficient to change the column headings here only. In some cases they can only be changed here.

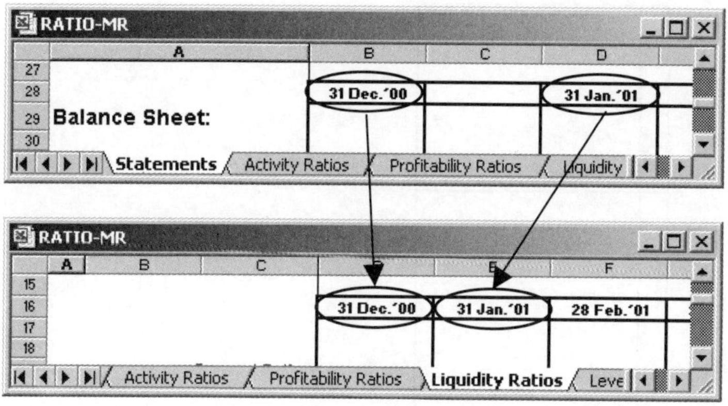

Fig. 6.5 - Showing how changes made to the column headings in the "Statements" worksheet are reflected automatically in other relevant worksheets.

Fig. 6.6 shows a data entry form for Income Statement & Balance Sheet data for each operational year, by quarters. Text in the areas shaded grey can be changed. Names on the worksheet written in blue (which is not visible in Fig. 6.6) may not be changed. Changing these names may change the definition and significance of individual indicators.

Company: **My Company Ltd.**
Year: **2001**
Amounts in: **GBP**

Income Statement:

	Q1		Q2		6 months		Q3		9 months		Q4	
	Actual	Forecast	**Actual**	Forecast	**Actual**	Forecast	**Actual**	Forecast	**Actual**	Forecast	**Actual**	Forecast
Net Sales:												
Costs and Expenses:	**0**	0	**0**	0			**0**	0			**0**	0
Labour and materials												
Other operating expenses												
Marketing and sales												
Research and development												
General and administrative												
Depreciation												
Interest expense												
Taxes												
Net Income:	**0**	0	**0**	0			**0**	0			**0**	0

Balance Sheet:

	31 Dec. '00	**31 Mar. '01**	**30 Jun. '01**	**30 Sep. '01**	**31 Dec. '01**
Total Current Assets	**0**	**0**	**0**	**0**	**0**
Accounts receivable					
Inventories					
Other					
Total Fixed Assets	**0**	**0**	**0**	**0**	**0**
Properties					
Equipment					
Other					
Total Assets:	**0**	**0**	**0**	**0**	**0**
Total Current Liabilities					
Total Long-Term Debt					
Total Liabilities:	**0**	**0**	**0**	**0**	**0**
Shareholders' Equity	**0**	**0**	**0**	**0**	**0**
Common Stock					
Retained earnings					
Total Liabilities and Shareholders' Equity:	**0**	**0**	**0**	**0**	**0**

Fig. 6.6 - The worksheet for entry of Income Statement and Balance Sheet data for each operational year, by quarters.

The name of the company is at the top of the worksheet, together with the year being analysed and the currency in which sums are entered.

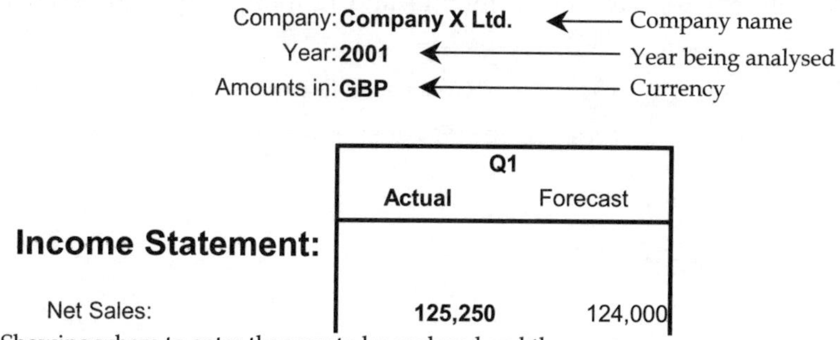

Fig. 6.7 - Showing where to enter the year to be analysed and the currency.

Income Statement

The operational year is divided into the following columns:

- 1st quarter (Q1 - 3 months)
- 2nd quarter (Q2 - 3 months)
- 6 months (sum of Q1 and Q2)
- 3rd quarter (Q3 - 3 months)
- 9 months (sum of Q3 and 6 months)
- 4th quarter (Q4 - 3 months)
- 12 months (sum of Q4 and 9 months)

The operational year is divided into quarters, which are summed after 6, 9 and 12 months. Each quarter reflects the actual outcome (or forecast) for 3 months at a time, while in the summation values the quarters are added together, so showing the outcome (or forecast) from the beginning of the operational year.

If the operating balance is made only at six-monthly intervals, then the figure for the first half of the year should be entered in the space for the 2nd quarter and that for the second half of the year in the space for the 4th quarter.

The columns for 6 months, 9 months and 12 months may not be changed.

The spaces for figures under "Costs and Expenses" and "Net income" may not be changed, as they are spaces for sum totals.

Balance Sheet

The balance is divided into 5 periods:

- The end of the previous operational year (generally 31st Dec. of the previous year).
- The end of the first quarter (generally 31st March each year).
- The end of the second quarter (generally 30th June each year).
- The end of the third quarter (generally 30th September each year).
- The end of the fourth quarter (generally 31st December each year).

It is important to enter the balance for the end of the previous operational year, as it forms the basis for the DuPont analysis, and many other indicators are calculated on the basis of the position at the beginning of the year (the capital position at the beginning of the operational year).

The cells for figures under "Current assets", "Fixed assets", "Total assets", "Total liabilities", "Equity" and "Total equity and liabilities" may not be changed, as they are cells for sum totals.

TIP Companies whose operational year does not coincide with the calendar year can use the model by making new headings for the periods.

6.1.3 Calculation of ratios

The indicators are divided into four groups:

- Activity ratios.
- Profitability ratios.
- Liquidity ratios.
- Leverage ratios

There is a separate worksheet for each group. An explanation of the indicators in each group appears at the head of each sheet:

2. Operating Profit Margin:	**4. Return on Stockholders' Equity (ROE):**
Formula: $\frac{\text{Earnings before interest \& taxes}}{\text{Sales}}$	**Formula:** $\frac{\text{Net profit after taxes}}{\text{Total stockholders' equity}}$
Indication: Shows profitability of basic operations	**Indication:** Shows return on stockholders' investment

Fig. 6.8 - Examples of the boxes at the head of the worksheet for each group.

The explanations begin with the name of the indicator, followed by the formula and a short description of the meaning of the indicator.

All calculations involving forecasts are based on the balance at the end of the previous operational year. This is done so as to make it possible to calculate indicators immediately based on the balance at the time that the budget was made.

TIP If the balance is not yet available, it can be estimated on the basis of available data. Then the registered value is updated when the Balance Sheet is drawn up.

Activity ratios

Basic document: RATIO-QR.XLS
Worksheet: Activity Ratios

Fig. 6.9 shows activity ratios. The model calculates all the ratios automatically; thus it is not possible to change any of the cells on the worksheet.

The following ratios are calculated:

- Inventory Turnover.
- Inventory Average Collection (days).
- Fixed Assets Turnover.
- Total Assets Turnover.
- Accounts Receivable Turnover.
- Accounts Receivable Average Collection (days).

Activity ratios are calculated on the basis of both Income Statement and Balance Sheet figures.

1. Inventory Turnover:

Formula: $\frac{\text{Sales}}{\text{Average Inventory}}$

Indication: Shows capital tied up in inventories in terms of sales

2. Inventory Average Collection (days):

Formula: $\frac{365}{\text{Inventory turnover (\%)}}$

Indication: The number of days a company takes to collect revenues for sales granted on inventories

3. Accounts Receivable Turnover:

Formula: $\frac{\text{Sales}}{\text{Average accounts receivable}}$

Indication: Shows capital tied up in accounts receivable in terms of sales

4. Accounts Receivable Average Collection (days)

Formula: $\frac{365}{\text{Accounts receivable turnover (\%)}}$

Indication: The number of days a company takes to collect revenues for sales granted on credit

5. Fixed Assets Turnover:

Formula: $\frac{\text{Sales}}{\text{Average fixed assets}}$

Indication: Reflects the extent to which plant, equipment and machinery are utilized

6. Total Assets Turnover:

Formula: $\frac{\text{Sales}}{\text{Average total assets}}$

Indication: Shows utilisation of all the company's assets

	Q1		Q2		6 months		Q3		9 months		Q4	
	Actual	Forecast	**Actual**	Forecast	**Actual**	Forecast	**Actual**	Forecast	**Actual**	Forecast	**Actual**	Forecast
Inventory Turnover:												
Period of operation:												
On an annual basis:												
Inventory Average Collect. (D):												
Period of operation:												
Fixed Assets Turnover:												
Period of operation:												
On an annual basis:												
Total Assets Turnover:												
Period of operation:												
On an annual basis:												
Account Receivable Turnover:												
Period of operation:												
On an annual basis:												
Acc. Receiv. Avg. Collect. (D):												
Period of operation:												

Fig. 6.9 - Activity ratios.

Profitability ratios

Basic document: **RATIO-QR.XLS**
Worksheet: **Profitability Ratios**

Fig. 6.10 shows the profitability ratios. The model calculates all the ratios automatically; thus it is not possible to change any of the cells on the worksheet.

The following ratios are calculated:

- Operating Profit Margin
- Return on Sales (ROS)
- Return on Total Assets (ROA)
- Return on Stockholders' Equity (ROE)
- Earnings per Share (EPS)

The Operating Profit Margin and ROS are based on the outcome of the Income Statement. The other ratios are calculated on the basis of both Income Statement and Balance Sheet figures.

1. Return on Sale (ROS):

Formula: $\frac{\text{Net profit after taxes}}{\text{Sales}}$

Indication: Shows profit in relation to sales

2. Operating Profit Margin:

Formula: $\frac{\text{Earnings before interest \& taxes}}{\text{Sales}}$

Indication: Shows profitability of basic operations

3. Return on Total Assets (ROA):

Formula: $\frac{\text{Net profit after taxes}}{\text{Total assets}}$

Indication: Shows profit in relation to investments in assets

4. Return on Stockholders' Equity (ROE):

Formula: $\frac{\text{Net profit after taxes}}{\text{Total stockholders' equity}}$

Indication: Shows return on stockholders' investment

5. Earnings per Share (EPS):

Formula: $\frac{\text{Net profit after taxes}}{\text{Common stock}}$

Indication: Shows profit per common stock unit

	Q1		Q2		6 months		Q3		9 months		Q4	
	Actual	Forecast	**Actual**	Forecast	**Actual**	Forecast	**Actual**	Forecast	**Actual**	Forecast	**Actual**	Forecast
Operating Profit Margin:												
Period of operation:												
Return on Sale (ROS):												
Period of operation:												
Return on Total Assets (ROA):												
Period of operation:												
On an annual basis:												
Return on Equity (ROE):												
Period of operation:												
On an annual basis:												
Earnings per Share (EPS):												
Period of operation:												
On an annual basis:												

Fig. 6.10 - Profitability ratios.

Liquidity ratios

Basic document: RATIO-QR.XLS
Worksheet: Liquidity Ratios

Fig. 6.11 shows liquidity ratios. The model calculates all the ratios automatically; thus it is not possible to change any of the cells on the worksheet.

The following ratios are calculated:

- Current Ratio.
- Quick Ratio.

Liquidity ratios are calculated solely on the basis of Balance Sheet figures; hence they are calculated each time a Balance Sheet is drawn up.

1. Current Ratio:	2. Quick Ratio:
Formula: $\frac{\text{Current assets}}{\text{Current liabilities}}$	**Formula:** $\frac{\text{Current assets - Inventories}}{\text{Current liabilities}}$
Indication: The ability to meet short-term obligations	**Indication:** The ability to meet short-term obligations without needing to depend on sale of inventories

	31 Dec.'00	31 Mar. '01	30 Jun. '01	30 Sep. '01	31 Dec. '01
Current Ratio:					
Quick Ratio:					

Fig. 6.11 - Liquidity ratios.

Leverage ratios

Basic document: RATIO-QR.XLS
Worksheet: Leverage Ratios

Fig. 6.12 shows the leverage ratios of a company. The model calculates all the ratios automatically; thus it is not possible to change any of the cells on the worksheet.

The following ratios are calculated:

- Equity Ratio.
- Book Value per Common Stock (rate 1.0 = nominal value).

Leverage ratios are calculated solely on the basis of Balance Sheet figures; hence they are calculated each time a Balance Sheet is drawn up.

1. Equity Ratio:	2. Book Value per Common Stock:
Formula: Shareholders' equity / Total liabilities and shareholders' equit	**Formula:** Shareholders' equity / Common stock
Indication: Reveals the percentage of total funds supplied by shareholders	**Indication:** Reveals the value of common stock according to the balance sheet. Not necessarily the market value.

	31 Dec.'00	31 Mar. '01	30 Jun. '01	30 Sep. '01	31 Dec. '01
Equity ratio:					
Book value per common stock:					

Fig. 6.12 - Leverage ratios.

6.2 Ratio Analysis of Trends

6.2.1 Entry of data in the "Statements" worksheet

Basic document: **RATIO-YL.XLS**
Worksheet: **Statements**

Fig. 6.14 shows the data sheet for the trend analysis of Income Statement and Balance Sheet figures. The sheet is similar to the data sheet for Annual Ratio Analysis explained in Section 6.1. Terms written in blue on the worksheet (not distinguished in Fig. 6.13) should not be altered. Changes made to their contents may alter the meaning of individual ratios.

The header is identical to the header of the data sheet for Annual Ratio Analysis. The name of the company and the amount / currency units used appear at the top of the worksheet (see Fig. 6.13).

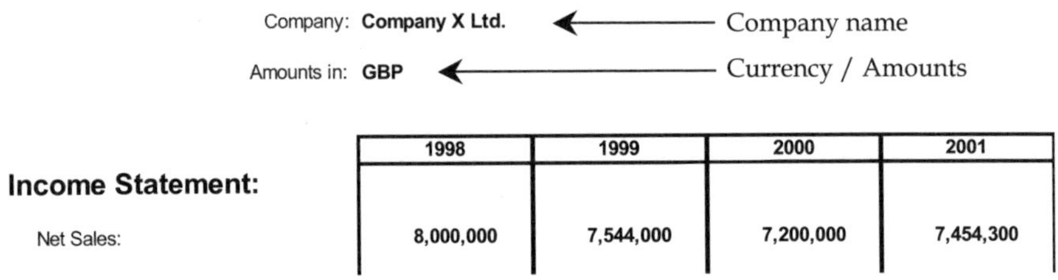

Fig. 6.13 - Showing the name of the company. The currency to be used should be entered here.

Company: **My Company Ltd.**

Amounts in: **GBP**

Income Statement:

	1994	1995	1996	1997	1998	1999	2000	2001	2002	2003	2004	2005
Net Sales:												
Costs and Expenses:	0	0	0	0	0	0	0	0	0	0	0	0
Labour and materials												
Other operating expenses												
Marketing and sales												
Research and development												
General and administrative												
Depreciation												
Interest expense												
Taxes												
Net Income:	0	0	0	0	0	0	0	0	0	0	0	0

Balance Sheet:

	31 Dec. 1994	31 Dec. 1995	31 Dec. 1996	31 Dec. 1997	31 Dec. 1998	31 Dec. 1999	31 Dec. 2000	31 Dec. 2001	31 Dec. 2002	31 Dec. 2003	31 Dec. 2004	31 Dec. 2005
Total Current Assets	0	0	0	0	0	0	0	0	0	0	0	0
Accounts receivable												
Inventories												
Other												
Total Fixed Assets	0	0	0	0	0	0	0	0	0	0	0	0
Properties												
Equipment												
Other												
Total Assets:	0	0	0	0	0	0	0	0	0	0	0	0
Total Current Liabilities												
Total Long-Term Debt												
Total Liabilities:	0	0	0	0	0	0	0	0	0	0	0	0
Shareholders' Equity	0	0	0	0	0	0	0	0	0	0	0	0
Common Stock												
Retained earnings												
Total Liabilities and Shareholders' Equity:	0	0	0	0	0	0	0	0	0	0	0	0

Fig. 6.14 - The worksheet for entry of Income Statement and Balance Sheet data for Trend analysis.

Income Statement and Balance Sheet figures

Only actual figures from the end of each operational year are to be entered. Thus, the model can be used to examine changes in operational figures and ratios over periods of up to 14 years at a time.

As before, the Income Statement data, the "Costs and Expenses" and "Net Income" cells may not be altered, as they are summation cells. The same goes for the Balance Sheet data, the "Total Current Assets", "Total Fixed Assets", "Total Assets", "Total Liabilities", "Shareholders' Equity" and "Liabilities and Shareholders' Equity". These cells may not be altered, as they are summation cells.

6.2.2 Calculation of ratios

Ratio Analysis of Trends is in principle identical to Annual Ratio Analysis. The difference is that calculation of a ratio for the operational period is the same value as the annualised value.

This means that only one value is calculated for each, instead of two as is the case with ratios for quarters and months (i.e. for operational periods and on an annualised basis - see Section 6.1).

6.3 DuPont Analysis

Basic documents: RATIO-YR.XLS, RATIO-QR.XLS, RATIO-MR.XLS
Worksheet: DuPont

The DuPont Model consists of three units:

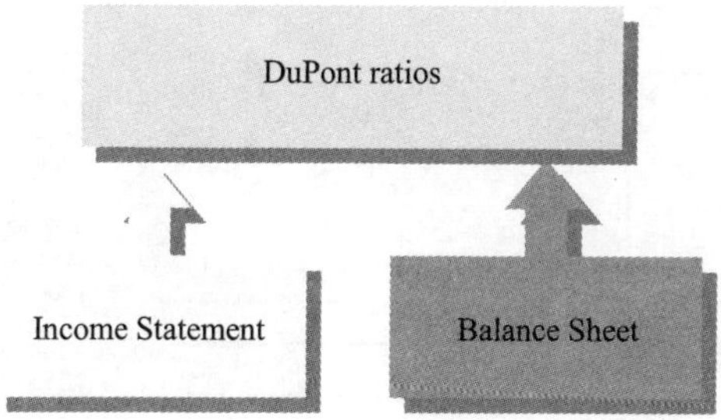

Fig. 6.15 - The three main units of the DuPont Model.

Each unit has a special colour in the model to distinguish it from the others. It is not recommended that these colours be changed, as they have been chosen to ensure the best results in printing, both in colour and in black and white.

As can be seen from Fig. 6.15, the DuPont Model consists of a pyramid. The basic data from the Income Statement and Balance Sheet are combined in the Profitability Ratios, which produce the Return on Stockholders' Equity ratio (ROE).

Each box in the DuPont Model contains a heading and two numerical values, the upper one being the value for the operational period selected, the lower being an annualised value.

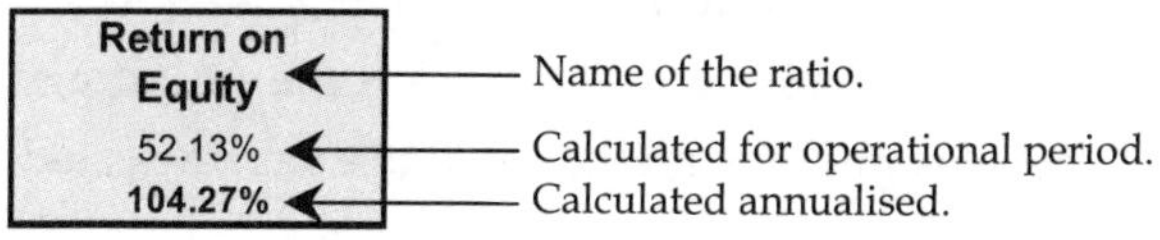

Fig. 6.16 - Structure of each box in the DuPont Model.

The DuPont Model can be displayed for all operational periods. There is a pull-down menu on the DuPont worksheet offering a choice of various periods for processing.

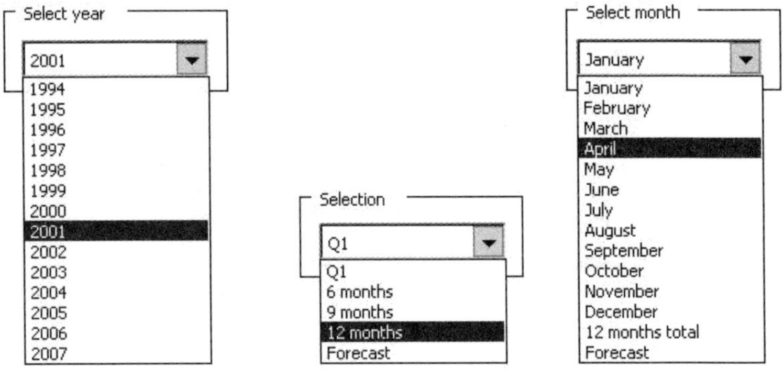

Ratios for years | Ratios for quarters | Ratios for months

Fig. 6.17 - Showing how various periods are chosen in the DuPont Model.

If the headings of the operational periods on the "Statement" worksheet are changed, then the headings in the DuPont Model will also be changed.

Fig. 6.18 shows the DuPont Model. All ratios in the DuPont Model are calculated automatically. All Income Statement and Balance Sheet values in the DuPont Model can be changed by writing figures straight into the appropriate number cells, thus carrying out a "what if" analysis.

When values have been written in over previous values in the DuPont Model, the original values can be restored by choosing a new period from the pull-down menu. If a "what if" analysis is made for a particular period and it is necessary to restore the original values for the same period, another period must first be selected from the pull-down menu and then the period that was under examination must be re-selected.

TIP The balance in the DuPont Model is always based on the balance at the beginning of the year. Thus the Total Assets Turnover in the DuPont Model is not the same figure as the Return on Total Assets (ROA) ratio, which is based on an average for the period.

The boxes for the quarterly ratios each contain two figures. The upper is the outcome figure for the period, and the lower is the annualised outcome.

The annualised outcome shows the outcome for the year if operations continue on the same path as during the operational period under examination.

The left part of the diagram contains operational items, showing the main expense categories with the conclusion, net income, remaining after the deduction of operating expenses.

On the right side of the diagram is the Balance Sheet. Total assets are the sum of fixed and current assets. The diagram shows the further breakdown of each of these two categories. As has already been stated, the balance sheet items in the DuPont Model represent the situation at the beginning of the operational period, i.e. the capital that was used for operations.

The upper part of the diagram shows the formation of various ratios that have already been discussed. The return on sale is produced by dividing net income by net sales. Total assets turnover is obtained by dividing net sales by assets. Return on total assets is the multiple of the return on sale and total assets turnover. The return on equity in terms of the return on total assets is obtained by multiplying the return on total assets by the ratio total assets/equity.

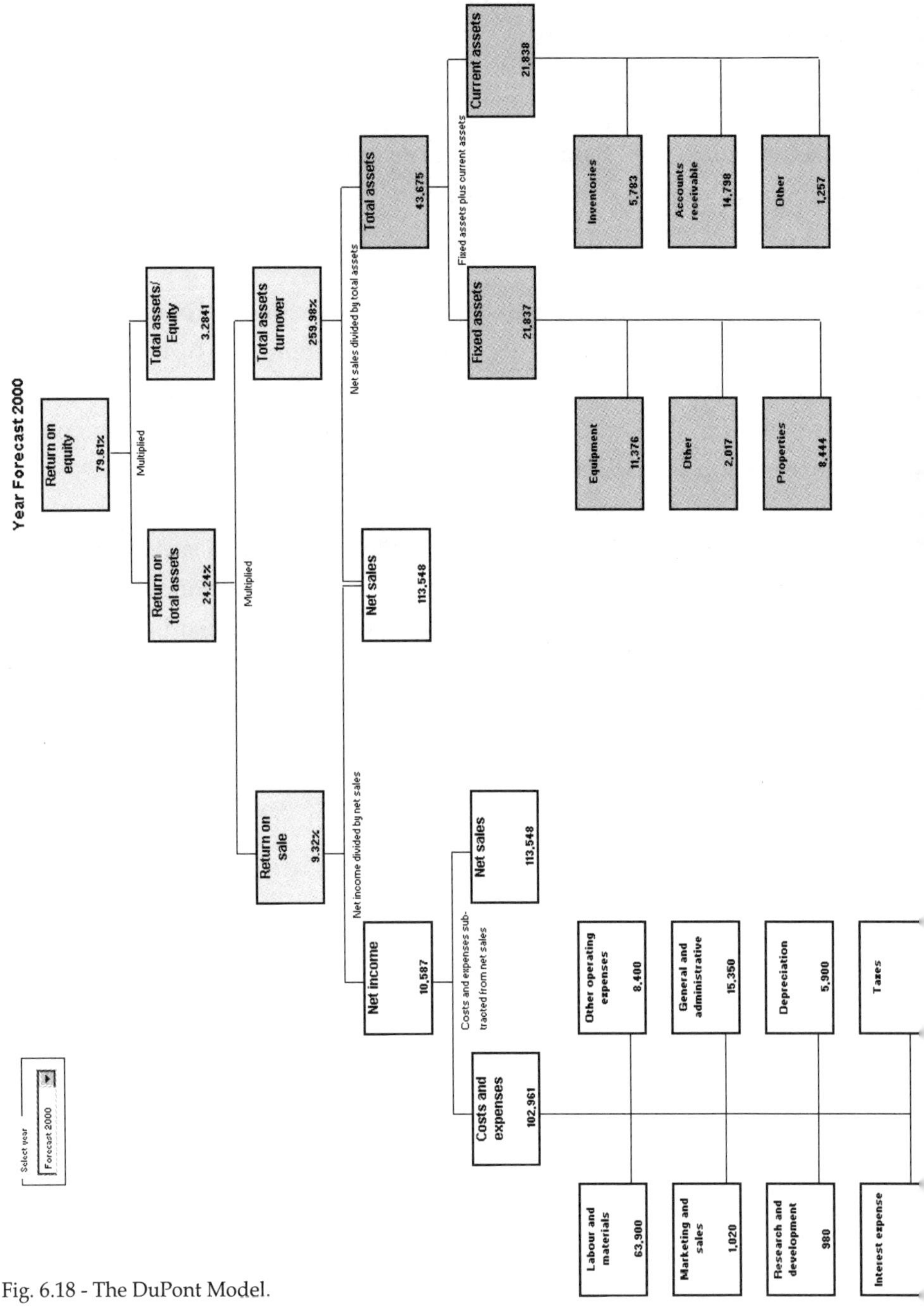

Fig. 6.18 - The DuPont Model.

6.4 Graphical Presentation

Basic documents: RATIO-YG.XLS, RATIO-QG.XLS, RATIO-MG.XLS
Worksheet: GraphData

The following standard graphs are included in the system:

- Profits after tax.
- Income and expenses.
- Equity.
- Assets.
- Liabilities.
- Current assets.
- Profitability.
- Return on investments and equity.
- Return per share.
- Total assets turnover.
- Inventory turnover.
- Accounts receivable turnover.
- Liquidity.
- Equity ratio.
- Book value per common stock.

Each graph has its own worksheet, and can be displayed by selecting the tab. The graphs are printed in the same way as other worksheets.

Generally speaking, the same explanations apply to the graph documents for all three models (months, quarters, years).

Graphs for quarters and months show the changes within the operational year. The graphs are updated automatically when changes are made to the Income Statement and Balance Sheet data in the data document. If changes are made to certain aspects of the appearance of the graphs (see "Drawing graphs" below), then the graphs will have to be redrawn.

Graphs based on annual figures show changes or trends from year to year. All data on which the graphs are based are revised automatically when changes are made to the Income Statement and Balance Sheet data in the "Statements" worksheet.

The graphs are updated automatically to a certain extent. The standard graphs are drawn to cover periods of five years. If the user wishes to reduce or increase the number of years covered, the graphs will have to be redrawn. For example, if the graphs have been drawn for the years 1999-2000, and the figures for 2001 then become available, then all the graphs will have to be redrawn to include 2001 (see "Drawing graphs" below).

Drawing graphs

If the number of years or one or more of the following items (see Fig. 6.19) on a graph are changed, then the graph will have to be redrawn:

- The title.
- The legend on the X-axis.
- The legend on the Y-axis.
- The type of graph.
- The name of the worksheet.

To draw graphs, select the cells containing material to be drawn as shown in Fig. 6.19.

15	Graph definition:				
16	Title:	Sales and expenses			
17	Type:	Line			
18	Worksheet:	Sales&exp			
19	y-axis	GBP			
20	x-axis	Year			
21					
22		1998	1999	2000	2001
23	Net sales	8,000,000	7,544,000	7,200,000	7,454,300
24	Costs and expenses	6,210,000	6,976,800	5,449,545	5,294,545
25					

Fig. 6.19 - Selecting the cells containing data to be used on a graph.

The years at the top of the columns must be included in the data selected to be used on the graph (see Fig. 6.19).

To draw the graph, select "Draw graph" from the "Model" menu.

It makes no difference whether all the lines, or only particular cells, are selected. But the cells must be selected specially if operational years covered by the period have a zero value (e.g. if data are not available for two or more years).

Chapter 7 Using Models for Strategic Ratio Analysis

7.1 Future Development of the Equity Ratio

7.1.1 Model: ER-Prop.xls

The program consists of three parts: "**CSF Evaluation**", "**Equity-Ratio Proposals**" and "**Graph**".

The "CSF Evaluation" part prompts the user to evaluate and weight a number of statements by inserting weightings from 1 - 10 indicating the factors that are of the greatest importance for the company. "Evaluation" here means the importance of the issue in question. If, for instance, "frequency of changes in fashion" is evaluated as being of absolutely no importance to the company, it is given a value of 1; if, on the other hand, it is considered to be vital, it is given a value of 10.

Next, it is necessary to give a weighting to each heading. If, for instance, frequency of changes in fashion has been evaluated as important for the company with, for example, a value of 8, and the frequency of change is estimated at 1 to 2 years, there are two possibilities for weighting, i.e. 7 or 8. Whether the changes take place at intervals closer to 1 or 2 years will determine the weighting. If changes occur at intervals close to 1 year, the weighting will be 8, whereas intervals closer to 2 years will give a weighting of 7.

The program will then correlate the evaluation and the weighting to produce a score for each factor, and these individual scores will be summed to produce a Total Score.

The philosophy behind the program is that a number of factors are important for the choice of goal for the Equity Ratio. The more important the factor is and the more it influences the capacity of survival of the company, the higher the Equity Ratio should be. This means that a high Total Score will call for a high Equity Ratio.

Critical Success Factor Evaluation:

0 = Absolutely no value
1 = No practical value
2 = Not important
3 = Small influence
4 = Some importance but not critical
5 = Important but not critical
6 = Important and sometimes critical
7 = Very important
8 = Extremely important
9 = Critical for future operation
10 = Vital for the company

Critical Success Factors:	Evaluation	Weighting: 1 or 2	Weighting: 3 or 4	Weighting: 5 or 6	Weighting: 7 or 8	Weighting: 9 or 10	Total Score (CSF Evaluation x Weighting)
Market:							
The client base	7	No one > 2% of sales	Few > 2%, No one > 5% of sales	Few > 5%, No one > 10% of sales	Many > 5%, No one > 10% of sales 7	Many > 10% of sales	49
Clients stability	8	Old clients > 90%	Old clients > 75%	Old clients > 60% 5	New clients > 70%	New clients > 80%	40
Industry / market stability:							
Frequency of changes in fashion	4	5 years or more	3 - 5 years	2 - 3 years	1 - 2 years	Less than 1 year 10	40
Market response	6	Stable market	Slow reaction from the market 4	Normal reaction from the market	Quick reaction from the market	Very fast reaction from the market	24
Annual market growth	7	Ageing market, negative growth	Stable market, 0-growth	Moderate growth, 0-5% growth	Growth > 5% < 10%	Growth > 10% 9	63
New markets	3	Not actual within the next 3 years	Actual within the next 3 years	Normal expansion policy 6	Necessary to maintain position	Necessary to maintain income	18
Products:							
Technology development	3	Prod. Methods have no or little importance	Prod. methods used for over 10 years	Prod. meth. > 5 years but < 10 years 5	Radical changes within 5 years	Radical changes within 3 years	15
Product life-cycle	9	Prod. life-cycle > 6 years	Prod. life-cycle > 4 years < 6 years	Prod. life-cycle > 2 years < 4 years	Prod. life-cycle < 2 years 7	Prod. life-cycle < 6 months	63
Product usage	6	Not price sensitive	Price sensitivity < +- 5%	5 % <Price sensitivity< 10 % 5	Price sensitivity > 10 %	Price sensitivity extreme	30
Products or prod meth. influencing the environment	8	No influence upon the environment	Influence upon enviornment small	Polluting, but not critical	Polluting 8	Highly polluting	64
Employees:							
Recruiting	9	Direct access to qualified resources 1	Resources available	Resources available but expencive	Resources scarce	No resources available	9
Mobility	7	Mobility not possible	Difficult to moove 3	Normal turnover	Large degree of turnover	Labourforce unstable	21
Internal training	6	Training not necessary 1	Training worthwhile but not necessary	Some training necessary	Training necessary and expensive	Extensive training needed	6
Suppliers:							
Substitution of suppliers	3	Many identical suppliers	Few but easy access to suppliers	Substitution possible but stock incr. 6	Substitution difficult and stock incr.	Substitution not possible	18
Quality of suppliers	8	Substit. with same quality possible	Substit. possible with but little loss of qual.	Substit. only possible with loss of quall. 6	Substit. only poss. With cons. Loss of quall.	Quality cannot be maintained	48
Capital structure:							
Assets turnover	4	Much better than industry	Better than industry	Equals average of industry 6	Less than average of industry	Far below average of industry	24
Interest rate	4	Stable 2	Small but insignificent fluctuations	Significant fluctuations	Significant and frequent fluctuations	Critical fluctuations	8
Sensitivity to level of interest rates	5	Interest rate has no or little bearing upon result	Interest rate influences result, but not critical	Interest rate influences result considerably 6	Interest rate highly important for result	Result critically depending upon interest rate	30
							570

Fig. 7.1 – The Critical Success Factors Evaluation Sheet.

		ER Goal		Branch Average Equity Ratio:	Industry Average Equity Ratio:
		0.36		0.30	0.37
Scale:	**Variable:**	**Total Score Interval:** Your score: 570		**Proposal:**	**Proposal:**
1	1.00	0	180	0.30	0.37
2	1.05	181	360	0.32	0.39
3	1.10	361	540	0.33	0.41
4	**1.15**	**541**	**720**	0.35	0.43
5	1.20	721	900	0.36	0.44
6	1.25	901	1080	0.38	0.46
7	1.30	1081	1260	0.39	0.48
8	1.40	1261	1440	0.42	0.52
9	1.50	1441	1620	0.45	0.56
10	1.60	1620	1800	0.48	0.59

Fig. 7.2a - Calculation of Equity Ratio Proposals

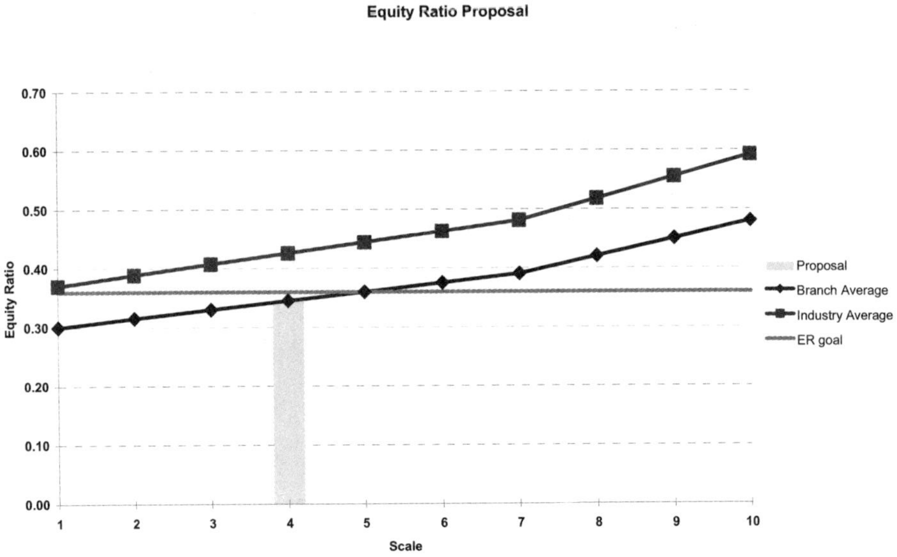

Fig. 7.2b - Calculation of Equity Ratio Proposals

The factors chosen for the program are considered to be of general importance, but individual companies may face special conditions that are not included in the program. It is then advisable to replace some of the factors that are considered of little or no importance by some that are of more importance to the company, in which case it will be necessary to change the headings of the weightings.

The "Equity-Ratio Proposals" part calculates the proposed Equity Ratio. The sum of the product of the weightings and evaluations gives a Total Score which, together with the average Equity Ratio for the industry and branch, forms the basis for the Equity Ratio goal that the program will suggest, so these average values therefore have to be inserted. The proposed Equity Ratio is indicated in intervals, depending upon the Total Score and the averages inserted. As will be noticed, the program does not indicate any value below the inserted averages, simply because it is never advisable to have a goal for the Equity Ratio that is lower than the average for industry or branch.

It also must be realised that the value suggested by the program is based on the input values and does not reflect the wishes or intuitive opinions of the owners or managers. Nor is it always possible to adopt the program's suggestion, and the company may be in a situation in which short-term growth is preferred to an acceptable Equity Ratio for strategic reasons. The final choice the Equity Ratio goal therefore must be influenced by these factors, but although short-term deviations from the suggested value might be acceptable, long-range deviations upward or downward should be considered very cautiously.

If for some reason the management of the company considers the program's suggested value is unrealistic or unacceptable, it is advisable to consider some of the factors influencing the suggestion, e.g.:

- Would it be possible to spread sales in such a way that even big clients have a lower proportion of the turnover?
- Would it be possible to create a higher degree of loyalty among clients, so that sales to old clients would increase to a higher level?
- Would it be possible to postpone exploitation of new markets?
- Would it be possible to influence the product's life-cycle?
- Would it be possible to alter the price sensitivity?

If none of these factors can be altered, then other measures described in the following programs must be taken.

7.1.2 Model: ER-Value.xls

ER-Value.xls. consists of two models: **"ER Dev. Static"** and **"ER Dev. dynamic"**, plus two corresponding graphs.

The model is a tool to analyse different key ratio scenarios with the aim of predicting the future development of the Equity Ratio.

Explanation of the three different Equity Ratios used in the model is to be found in Sections 3.2 and 4.2. The Equity Ratio (ER) is the calculated actual Equity Ratio. The Equity Ratio goal (ER_g) is the Equity Ratio that is considered to be appropriate for the company, and the Equity Ratio limit (ER_n) is the value which the Equity Ratio will tend towards according to the ER_n formula.

ER Dev. static

In "ER Dev. Static", the ER goal is taken from the model "ER-prop.xls".

The conclusions of the model, i.e. the ratios "ER / Er_g" and "ER_n / Er_g" for each year, are linked to the ER-Pos.xls model. There the user is able to analyse these values in the context of future strategic actions. For a more detailed explanation of these ratios, see Section 7.1.3.

1. Capital Efficiency (CE)	3. Growth Rate (G):	5. Equity Ratio Limit (ERn):
Formula: $\frac{\text{Sales}}{\text{Total Assets}}$	**Formula:** $\frac{\text{Sales year (n+1)}}{\text{Sales year (n)}} - 1$	**Formula:** $\frac{\text{Sales * Capital efficiency}}{\text{Growth Rate}}$
Indication: Shows the utilization (turnover) of all the company's assets	**Indication:** Estimated future growth in sales, e.g. based on last year's growth rate	**Indication:**
2. Net Profit Rate (NPR):	**4. Equity Ratio (ER):**	
Formula: $\frac{\text{Net profit after taxes - dividends}}{\text{Sales}}$	**Formula:** $\frac{\text{Equity}}{\text{Total liabilities including equity}}$	
Indication: The profit ratio which is reinvested, i.e. remains in the company.	**Indication:** Reveals the percentage of total funds supplied by shareholders	

	Year 1	Year 2	Year 3	Year 4	Year 5	Year 6	Year 7	Year 8	Year 9	Year 10
Balance Sheet:										
Total Assets	**100.00**	107.00	114.49	122.50	131.08	140.26	150.07	160.58	171.82	183.85
Equity	**25.00**	27.94	31.09	34.46	38.06	41.92	46.05	50.46	55.19	60.25
Income Statement:										
Sales	**110.00**	117.70	125.94	134.75	144.19	154.28	165.08	176.64	189.00	202.23
Net Profit - Dividends	**2.75**	2.94	3.15	3.37	3.60	3.86	4.13	4.42	4.73	5.06
Ratios:										
Capital efficiency (CE) - Static	1.100	1.100	1.100	1.100	1.100	1.100	1.100	1.100	1.100	1.100
Net Profit Rate (NPR) - Static	0.025	0.025	0.025	0.025	0.025	0.025	0.025	0.025	0.025	0.025
Growth rate (G) - Static	**0.070**	0.070	0.070	0.070	0.070	0.070	0.070	0.070	0.070	0.070
Equity Ratio - Development:										
Equity Ratio Goal (ERg)	0.450	0.450	0.450	0.450	0.450	0.450	0.450	0.450	0.450	0.450
Equity Ratio (ER)	0.250	0.261	0.272	0.281	0.290	0.299	0.307	0.314	0.321	0.328
Equity Ratio Limit (ERn)	0.393	0.393	0.393	0.393	0.393	0.393	0.393	0.393	0.393	0.393
ER / ERg, ERn / ERg Ratios:										
ER / ERg	56%	58%	60%	63%	65%	66%	68%	70%	71%	73%
ERn / ERg	87%	87%	87%	87%	87%	87%	87%	87%	87%	87%

Fig. 7.3 – The ER-Value Static Sheet

ER Dev. Static operates with a fixed Net Profit Rate, Capital Efficiency and Growth Rate, which are calculated from the values of total assets, equity, sales, net profit and growth rate for year 0.

Example 1:

Values for year 0:

Total assets = 390

Equity = 75

Sales = 460

Net profit rate = 12

Growth rate = 10%

In the ER-Prop.xls model, the ER goal is defined as 45%

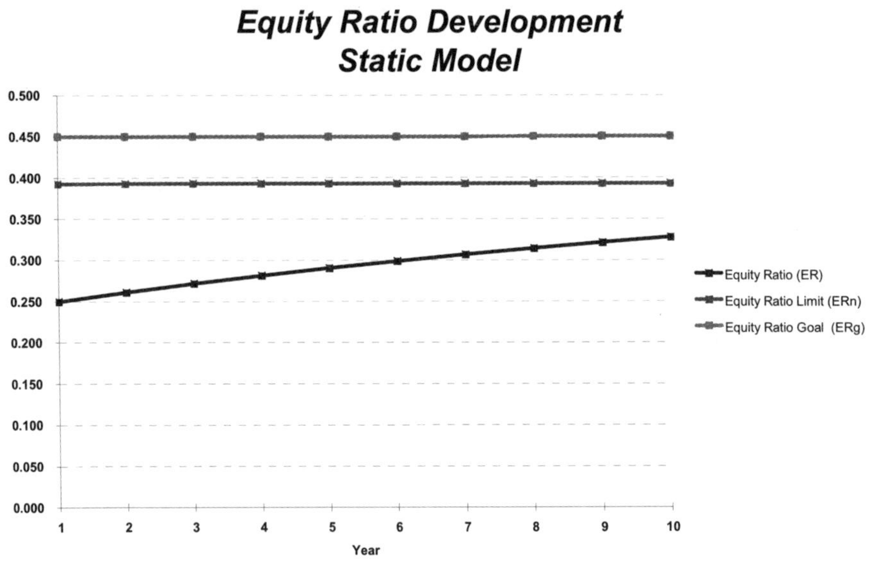

Figure 7.4 - Equity Ratio Development - Static Model.

The long-term development of the Equity Ratio, based on the above-mentioned values, is shown in Figure 7.4. As is indicated, the ER goal is a fixed value of 0.45. The ER limit is also a fixed value of 0.308 and the calculated Equity Ratio tends towards that value. This means that the company will never be able to raise its equity to the desired level on the basis of its operations. The first year the Equity Ratio is 19.2% and after 10 periods operation it will be 27.6% and tend towards 30.8%.

ER Dev. Dynamic allows a more detailed forecast, with values entered for each year and corrections made as necessary. The blue figures are calculated values; the black figures are those entered by the user.

The key values for year 0 that must be entered in the model are: total assets, equity, sales, net profit, growth rate, depreciation rate and the Equity Ratio goal.

ER Dev. dynamic

In ER Dev.dynamic, the Equity Ratio goal is not automatically taken from the ER-prop.xls model; it must be entered by the user. The depreciation rate is used to forecast the future value of total assets.

In the dynamic model, the user is able to add corrections to the calculated values of total assets and net profit. The "Real Net Profit" is simply the sum of the calculated value and the correction. The value of "Effective Total Assets" takes into account the effect of a sales increase on assets, and it also includes the correction entered by the user. Each addition of assets entered as correction is depreciated according to the depreciation rate defined. Each correction is thus modified for each year so the value of "Effective Total Assets" will be as realistic as possible.

As can be seen from the model, when the user enters different values for each year, the paths of ER_g, ER_n and calculated ER are not fixed, but change from one year to another. The desirable Equity Ratio for the company (the ER goal) may change from time to time. The different factors affecting the situation can be analysed in the "ER-prop" model. The value of the Equity Ratio limit and the relationship between it and the calculated ER should be interpreted as a given situation for each year.

1. Capital Efficiency (CE)

Formula: $\frac{\text{Sales}}{\text{Total Assets}}$

Indication: Shows utilisation of all the company's assets

2. Net Profit Rate (NPR):

Formula: $\frac{\text{Net profit after taxes - dividends}}{\text{Sales}}$

Indication: The profit ratio which is reinvested, i.e. remains in the company.

3. Growth Rate (G):

Formula: $\frac{\text{Sales year (n+1)}}{\text{Sales year (n)}} - 1$

Indication: Estimated future growth in sales, e.g. based on last year's growth rate

4. Equity Ratio (ER):

Formula: $\frac{\text{Equity}}{\text{Total liabilities including equity}}$

Indication: Reveals the percentage of total funds supplied by shareholders

5. Equity Ratio Limit (ERn):

Formula: $\frac{\text{Sales * Capital efficiency}}{\text{Growth Rate}}$

Indication:

	Year 1	Year 2	Year 3	Year 4	Year 5	Year 6	Year 7	Year 8	Year 9	Year 10
Balance Sheet:										
Total Assets	**100.00**	98.10	121.02	140.72	155.48	177.22	197.22	227.04	254.15	279.79
Total Assets Correction	**-10.00**	**15.00**	**0.00**	**0.00**	**5.00**	**0.00**	**10.00**	**0.00**	**0.00**	**15.00**
Effective Assets Correction	-10.00	15.00	10.50	7.35	10.15	7.10	14.97	10.48	7.34	20.14
Effective Total Assets	90.00	113.10	131.52	148.07	165.62	184.32	212.19	237.52	261.49	299.92
Equity	**25.00**	26.80	28.90	30.70	31.80	33.60	36.60	38.50	41.20	43.20
Income Statement:										
Sales	**110.00**	119.90	128.29	137.27	144.14	154.23	165.02	176.57	188.93	202.16
Net Profit - Dividends	**2.50**	**3.00**	**2.10**	**2.60**	**2.10**	**1.30**	**2.20**	**2.90**	**2.70**	**3.00**
Net Profit Correction	**-1.00**	**-1.20**	**ö.9**	**-0.80**	**-1.00**	**0.50**	**0.80**	**-1.00**	**ö.9**	**-1.00**
Real Net Profit	1.50	1.80	2.10	1.80	1.10	1.80	3.00	1.90	2.70	2.00
Ratios:										
Capital efficiency (CE) - Dynamic	1.222	1.060	0.975	0.927	0.870	0.837	0.778	0.743	0.723	0.674
Actual Capital Efficiency (ACE)	1.222	1.060	0.975	0.927	0.870	0.837	0.778	0.743	0.723	0.674
Net Profit Rate (NPR) - Dynamic	0.014	0.015	0.016	0.013	0.008	0.012	0.018	0.011	0.014	0.010
Growth rate (G) - Dynamic	**0.070**	**0.090**	**0.070**	**0.070**	**0.050**	**0.070**	**0.070**	**0.070**	**0.070**	**0.070**
Depreciation Rate	**0.300**	**0.300**	**0.300**	**0.300**	**0.300**	**0.300**	**0.300**	**0.300**	**0.300**	**0.300**
Equity Ratio - Development:										
Equity Ratio Goal (ERg)	**0.270**	**0.270**	**0.270**	**0.270**	**0.270**	**0.270**	**■.270**	**0.270**	**0.270**	**0.270**
Equity Ratio (ER)		0.273	0.239	0.218	0.205	0.190	0.186	0.170	0.162	0.154
Equity Ratio Limit (ERn)	0.238	0.177	0.228	0.174	0.133	0.140	C.202	0.114	0.148	0.095
ER / ERg, ERn / ERg Ratios:										
ER / ERg	0%	101%	88%	81%	76%	70%	69%	63%	60%	57%
ERn / ERg	88%	65%	84%	64%	49%	52%	75%	42%	55%	35%

Fig. 7.5 – The ER-Value Dynamic Sheet

7.1.3 Model: ER-Pos.xls

The model ER-Pos xls. is linked to ER-Value.xls. From the pull-down menu, the user can select data (assumptions) from the ER-Value model. This means that key ratios are moved from the ER-Value model and inserted into the formula of the ER-Pos model.

First the user selects either the static or the dynamic model from the ER-Value.xls, and then he selects year (1 - 10). The values given by this selection are shown at the top of the pull-down menu. The user can enter other values in the cells, which are then used for calculations. See Figure 7.6.

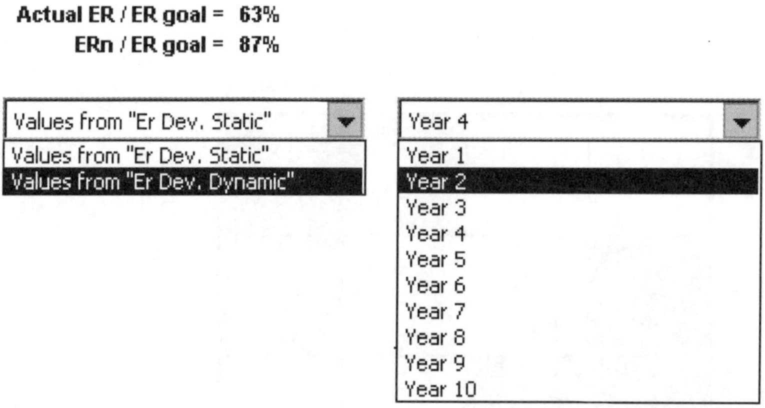

Figure 7.6 – Selection of values for calculations.

The ER-Pos model shows the company's position taking into consideration the calculated actual ER value and the ER_n compared to the Equity Ratio goal transferred from the ER-Value model. The program automatically places the company in a corresponding field. In the example shown in the table below the company has achieved between 40% and 70% of its ER goal and is heading towards an Equity Ratio between 70% and 100% of the goal. The program provides the user with evaluations of strategies and recommendations on measures to be taken in response to the position.

As will be noticed, the table is divided into rather broad intervals and so each interval spans some very different positions. For example, there is a big difference between having achieved 69% and 42% of the ER goal, just as there is a big difference between being about to achieve 72% or 99% of the goal. In the same way, there will be a difference depending upon whether the ER is rising or falling within the interval.

In cases where the company is positioned close to other intervals it is therefore recommended to check the descriptions and recommendations for these intervals. The only situation that does not call for any reaction is where the ER has reached the level of the target value or is rapidly approaching it.

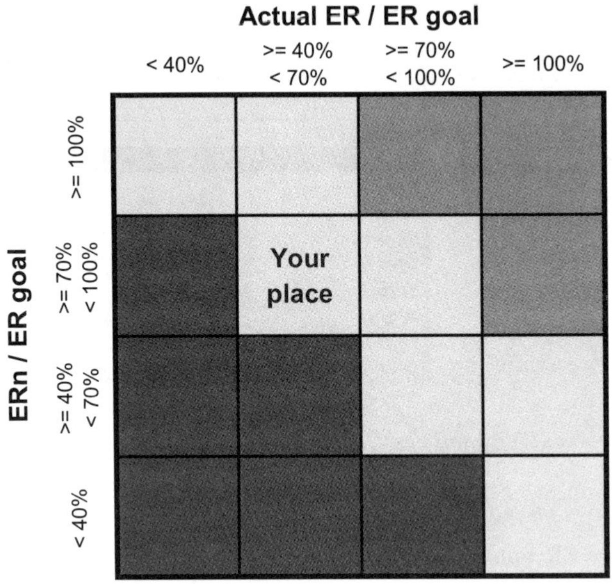

Figure 7.7 – The ER position matrix.

As is mentioned in the program, the descriptions and recommendations are general for the interval, and their importance for the company must be considered before action is taken.

Note when using the program that evaluations and recommendations do not automatically change if figures are altered, but that the "evaluations", "recommendations" or "both" must be used to take account of altered figures.

Appendix A contains printouts of evaluations and recommendations for all ER positions.

7.2 Strategic Budgeting

7.2.1 Model: S-Budget.xls

The model consists of two parts: "**Strat.Budg.Total"** and **"Strat.Budg. Detail"** and two worksheets containing graphs.

Sbudget.xls covers a period of 5 years and can be operated in two ways, either with the Total Capital Efficiency, Net Profit Rate and Growth Rate of the company (Strat.Budg.Total), which are easy to calculate, or on the basis of the Capital Efficiency, Net Profit Rate and Growth Rate of different customer/product groups, called segments (Strat.Budg.Detail). In the latter case, the Capital Efficiency and Net Profit Rate have to be calculated, and the Growth Rate must be inserted for each segment.

The Capital Efficiency, Net Profit Rate and Growth Rate can be kept constant throughout the whole budget period, in which case Future Sales are derived from Present Sales multiplied by (1 + actual Growth Rate for the year or years in question), and Future Total Assets are derived from Annual Sales divided by Capital Efficiency. It is generally believed that Capital Efficiency rises when Sales increase. Experience shows that this is not the case. Far more frequently, Capital Efficiency tends to be constant when Sales increase, while it tends to fall when there is a drop in Sales.

The strategic budget also can be operated by inserting the Capital Efficiency, Net Profit Rate and Growth Rate for each specific year; this course of action is recommended in cases where large fluctuations in the values are foreseen. Furthermore, it is possible to insert Sales, Net Profit and Total Assets for each year in question. In that case the automatic calculation of rates will be cancelled.

Calculation of the Capital Efficiency and Net Profit Rate for combinations of product/product groups and customer/customer groups is a difficult and time-consuming job, which in fact requires all costs, including fixed costs, and assets to be divided between products and/or customers. This task can be avoided in cases where only small alterations or adaptations are needed. Where the strategic budget indicates a highly dissatisfactory trend, a spread between customer/product - segments is needed.

Calculation of Capital Efficiency for each segment can be carried out through special analyses or by means of the models Calc-Sbudget.xls (U-values), or PM-Portfolio.xls. but these models only give relative figures for each segment, not absolute values.

The starting point for the procedure is year 0, and normally the closing balance for the previous year will be used, which in turn means that the equity, sales and total assets will be the same figures that have already been inserted in the inserted balance sheet.

An example of a strategic budget is shown below, based on the total Capital Efficiency, Net Profit Rate and Growth Rate of the company; these values are changed for each separate year. In the example the budget is, as mentioned, based on total CE, NPR and G Total Sales for the first year (Year 1) calculated as sales for the current year (Year 0) multiplied by (1 + G), in this example 1.055. Net Profit is calculated as total sales multiplied by NPR, in this case 1598 * 0.024 = 38.352. Equity for the first year is calculated as Equity for the current year + Net Profit for the first year, in this case 411 + 38 = 449. Total Assets are calculated as Sales divided by CE, in the example 1598/1.08 = 1479.63. ER is calculated as current equity divided by Total Assets. The ER-limit is calculated by means of the above-mentioned formula, CE * ER/G.

Company: **Company X Ltd.**

Amounts in: **GBP**

Strategic budget:

	Year 0	Year 1				Year 2			
	Results Y0	Cap. Eff.	N / ROS	Growth rate	**Results Y1**	Cap. Eff.	N / ROS	Growth rate	**Results Y2**
Key Figures:									
Annual Sales	**1,515**	**1.080**	**0.024**	**0.055**	1,598	**1.050**	**0.022**	**0.075**	1,718
Net profit					38				38
Equity	**411**				449				487
Total Assets	**1,263**				1,480				1,636
Equity Ratios:									
Equity Ratio - Budget	0.326				0.304				0.298
Equity Ratio - Limit	**0.330**				0.471				0.308
Equity Ratio - Goal					**0.350**				**0.360**

Figure 7.8a – The Strategic Budgeting Total Sheet

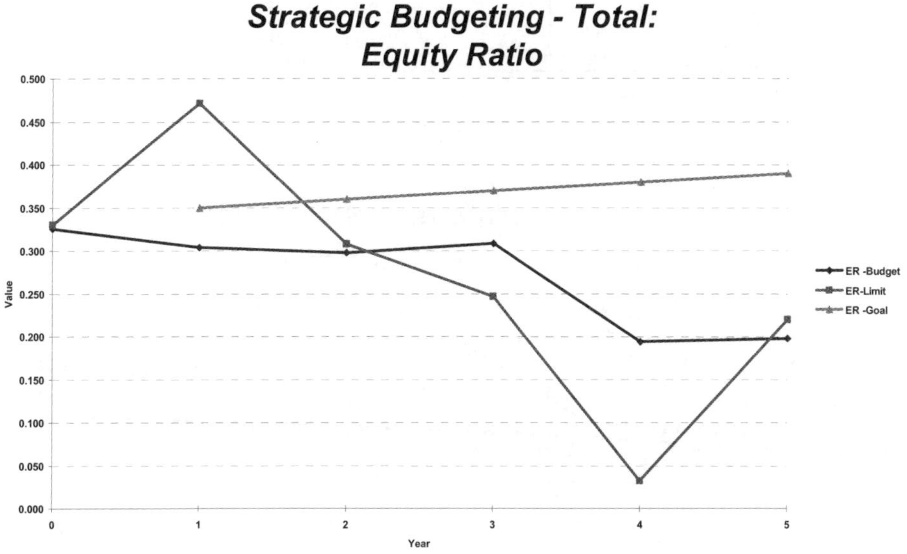

Figure 7.8b – The Strategic Budgeting Total Graph

Company: **Company X Ltd.**

Amounts in: **GBP**

Strategic budget:

	Year 0	Year 1				Year 2			
	Results	Cap. Eff.	N / ROS	Growth rate	Results Y1	Cap. Eff.	N / ROS	Growth rate	Results Y2
Segment analysis:	Annual sales				Annual sales				Annual sales
Segment 1:	125	1.100	0.030	0.080	135	1.150	0.030	0.100	149
Segment 2:	143	1.430	0.025	0.060	152	1.250	0.025	0.150	174
Segment 3:	94	1.540	0.035	0.050	99	1.540	0.035	0.200	118
Segment 4:	185	0.950	0.020	0.090	202	1.050	0.020	0.020	206
Segment 5:	65	1.350	0.040	0.100	72	1.150	0.040	0.100	79
Segment 6:	225	1.120	0.015	0.095	246	1.200	0.015	0.150	283
Segment 7:	157	0.850	0.011	0.110	174	0.850	0.011	0.000	174
Segment 8:	265	0.980	0.027	0.090	289	1.070	0.027	0.020	295
Segment 9:	135	1.270	0.033	0.065	144	1.270	0.033	0.150	165
Segment 10:	121	1.050	0.021	0.075	130	1.050	0.021	0.020	133
Total:	1,515	1.084	0.024	0.084	1,642	1.122	0.024	0.082	1,776
Key Figures:									
Net profit					39				43
Equity	411				450				493
Total Assets	1,263				1,515				1,583
Equity Ratios:									
Equity Ratio - Budget	0.326				0.297				0.311
Equity Ratio - Limit	0.330				0.308				0.329
Equity Ratio - Goal					0.350				0.360

Figure 7.9a – The Strategic Budgeting Detail Sheet

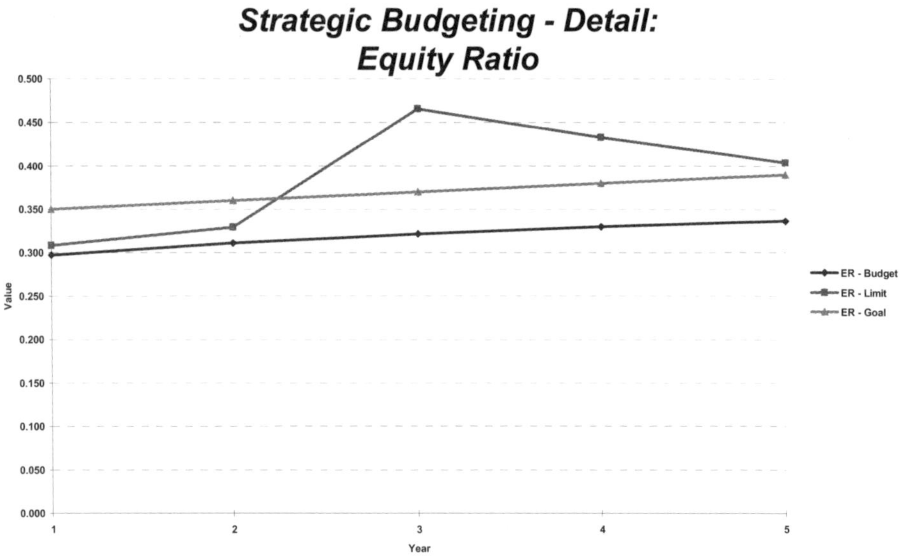

Figure 7.9b – The Strategic Budgeting Detail Graph

In the example, the first year brings a decrease in ER and a considerable increase in ER_n, which indicates that even though the first year's results must be considered highly unsatisfactory, future development along the same line as in year (n+1) would lead to a satisfactory result. However, the figures for year (n+2) show a decline in Capital Efficiency and the Net Profit Rate and an increase in the Growth Rate, which implies that both ER and ER_n are developing in a highly unsatisfactory direction and that measures must be taken either to increase Capital Efficiency or the Net Profit Rate or to reduce the Growth Rate, or to make changes in all three factors.

Company: **Company X Ltd.**

Amounts in: **GBP**

Strategic budget:

	Year 0	Year 1				Year 2			
	Results Y0	Cap. Eff.	N / ROS	Growth rate	**Results Y1**	Cap. Eff.	N / ROS	Growth rate	**Results Y2**
Key Figures:									
Annual Sales	**1,515**	**1.080**	**0.024**	**0.055**	1,598	**1.050**	**0.022**	**0.075**	1,718
Net profit					38				38
Equity	**411**				449				487
Total Assets	**1,263**				1,480				1,636
Equity Ratios:									
Equity Ratio - Budget	0.326				0.304				0.298
Equity Ratio - Limit	**0.330**				0.471				0.308
Equity Ratio - Goal					**0.350**				**0.360**

Figure 7.10 – Example 1.

In the Strat.Budg.Total model, the rows from 19 – 47 are grouped. The group is hidden / displayed by means of the "+" to the left of the worksheet. If the group is displayed, the program indicates what increase or reduction is necessary to initiate a satisfactory development, involving either an increase of Capital Efficiency or the Net Profit Rate or a reduction of the Growth Rate individually or combinations of increased Capital Efficiency and Net Profit Rate and reduced Growth Rate, or by other combinations that produce satisfactory results.

Nessecary values to achieve the Equity Ratio goal:

Equitybase = Year 0	in 1 year:	in 2 years (per year):	in 3 years (per year):	in 4 years (per year):	in 5 years (per year):
Change in NPR only (amount)	107	89	73	196	188
Change in NPR only (%)	0.067	0.054	0.042	0.091	0.075
Change in Capital efficiency only (%)	1.24				
Reduction in assets (amount)	196				
Relative reduction in assets (%)	13.2				

Equitybase = Year 1	in 1 year:	in 2 years (per year):	in 3 years (per year):	in 4 years (per year):
Change in NPR only (amount)	140	90	249	225
Change in NPR only (%)	0.081	0.050	0.106	0.083
Change in Capital efficiency only (%)	1.27			
Reduction in assets (amount)	283			
Relative reduction in assets (%)	17.3			

Equitybase = Year 2	in 1 year:	in 2 years (per year):	in 3 years (per year):
Change in NPR only (amount)	142	336	275
Change in NPR only (%)	0.076	0.126	0.090
Change in Capital efficiency only (%)	1.32		
Reduction in assets (amount)	283		
Relative reduction in assets (%)	16.7		

Equitybase = Year 3	in 1 year:	in 2 years (per year):
Change in NPR only (amount)	671	369
Change in NPR only (%)	0.194	0.102
Change in Capital efficiency only (%)	2.15	
Reduction in assets (amount)	1539	
Relative reduction in assets (%)	44.4	

Figure 7.11 – Rows 19 – 47 ungrouped.

It must be emphasised that any major deviation from the ER goal should be given careful consideration. A movement towards an ER of 0.471, when the goal has been set at 0.40, might indicate a lack of market- or product development. If this is not the case, then the set goal of 0.40 should be revised.

This unsatisfactory trend could be corrected by, e.g., ignoring the actual Growth Rate in the past. Instead, the Growth Rate could be set at 6% and the Net Profit Rate at 3% (a 50% increase in Net Profit Rate), or the Growth Rate and Net Profit rate could be maintained and the Capital Efficiency changed to 1.6 (a more than 30% reduction of assets, which would be unrealistic for most companies). The most realistic way to change the unsatisfactory trend would be to change all three denominators as shown below, where Capital Efficiency is increased to 1.2 and the Net Profit Rate to 2.3%, while the Growth Rate is set at 8%.

Company: **Company X Ltd.**

Amounts in: **GBP**

Strategic budget:

	Year 0	Year 1				Year 2				Year 3			
	Results Y0	Cap. Eff.	N / ROS	Growth rate	**Results Y1**	Cap. Eff.	N / ROS	Growth rate	**Results Y2**	Cap. Eff.	N / ROS	Growth rate	**Results Y3**
Key Figures:													
Annual Sales	**1,515**	**1.080**	**0.024**	**0.055**	1,598	**1.050**	**0.023**	**0.080**	1,726	**1,200.000**	**0.023**	**0.080**	1,864
Net profit					38				40				43
Equity	**411**				449				489				532
Total Assets	**1,263**				1,480				1,644				2
Equity Ratios:													
Equity Ratio - Budget	0.326				0.304				0.297				342.399
Equity Ratio - Limit	**0.330**				0.471				0.302				345.000
Equity Ratio - Goal					**0.350**				**0.360**				**0.370**

Figure 7.12 – Changes in Example 1.

However, methods other than changing the Capital Efficiency, Net Profit Rate and Growth Rate for the company as a whole are possible. To avoid an inordinate reduction in Total Assets or an unnecessary halt to total growth, the company tries to place growth upon customer/product segments whose Capital Efficiency or Net Profit Rate are above average, which might allow a higher Growth Rate. To demonstrate the effect of individual segments on the company's overall ER limit, use the model Sbudget.xls Detail. To carry out such procedures, however, requires a spread of Capital Efficiency, Net Profit Rate and Growth Rate between the individual customer/product segments, as is shown in the example below.

Company: **Company X Ltd.**

Amounts in: **GBP**

Strategic budget:

	Year 0	Year 1				Year 2				Year 3			
	Results	Cap. Eff.	N / ROS	Growth rate	**Results Y1**	Cap. Eff.	N / ROS	Growth rate	**Results Y2**	Cap. Eff.	N / ROS	Growth rate	**Results Y3**
Segment analysis:	**Annual sales**				**Annual sales**				**Annual sales**				**Annual sales**
Segment 1:	**125**	**1.100**	**0.030**	**0.080**	135	**1.150**	**0.030**	**0.100**	149	**1.150**	**0.020**	**0.000**	149
Segment 2:	**143**	**1.430**	**0.025**	**0.060**	152	**1.250**	**0.025**	**0.150**	174	**1.250**	**0.025**	**0.080**	188
Segment 3:	**94**	**1.540**	**0.035**	**0.050**	99	**1.540**	**0.035**	**0.200**	118	**1.540**	**0.025**	**0.100**	130
Segment 4:	**185**	**0.950**	**0.020**	**0.090**	202	**1.050**	**0.020**	**0.020**	206	**1.050**	**0.015**	**0.000**	206
Segment 5:	**65**	**1.350**	**0.040**	**0.100**	72	**1.150**	**0.040**	**0.100**	79	**1.150**	**0.030**	**0.000**	79
Segment 6:	**225**	**1.120**	**0.015**	**0.095**	246	**1.200**	**0.015**	**0.150**	283	**1.200**	**0.015**	**0.000**	283
Segment 7:	**157**	**0.850**	**0.011**	**0.110**	174	**0.850**	**0.011**	**0.000**	174	**0.850**	**0.020**	**0.000**	174
Segment 8:	**265**	**0.980**	**0.027**	**0.090**	289	**1.070**	**0.027**	**0.020**	295	**1.070**	**0.035**	**0.200**	354
Segment 9:	**135**	**1.270**	**0.033**	**0.065**	144	**1.270**	**0.033**	**0.150**	165	**1.270**	**0.025**	**0.000**	165
Segment 10:	**121**	**1.050**	**0.021**	**0.075**	130	**1.050**	**0.021**	**0.020**	133	**1.050**	**0.035**	**0.150**	153
Total:	1,515	1.084	0.024	0.084	**1,642**	1.122	0.024	0.082	**1,776**	1.122	0.024	0.059	**1,880**
Key Figures:													
Net profit					39				43				46
Equity	**411**				450				493				539
Total Assets	**1,263**				1,515				1,583				1,676
Equity Ratios:													
Equity Ratio - Budget	0.326				0.297				0.311				0.321
Equity Ratio - Limit	**0.330**				0.308				0.329				0.466
Equity Ratio - Goal					**0.350**				**0.360**				**0.370**

Figure 7.13 – Example 2.

As Example 2 shows, the same ER-limit as in Example 1 can be maintained at a higher growth rate by choosing segments with higher Capital Efficiency and/or Net Profit Rate, and consequently a higher ER-limit can be maintained at the same Growth Rate.

As shown, strategic budgeting offers the possibility of achieving the company's Equity Ratio goal by altering its Capital Efficiency, Net Profit Rate or Growth Rate, or by encouraging growth in those segments whose Capital Efficiency and Net Profit Rate are above average.

The procedure is simple: Enter the Capital Efficiency, Net Profit Rate and Growth Rate for each year in the model Sbudget.xls Total and adjust the denominators until a satisfactory result is achieved; then calculate the changes needed in absolute figures. Alternatively, enter the Capital Efficiency, Net Profit Rate and Growth Rate for each segment and each year in question in the model Sbudget.xls Detail and adjust the denominators until a satisfactory result is achieved.

7.3 Choice of Future Markets and Products

7.3.1 Model: PM-Portfolio.xls

As has already been mentioned, dividing fixed costs or assets between products or customers is a difficult and time-consuming and job that can be neither accurate nor objective. However, accuracy is not vital in selecting segments as a basis for growth: even rough approximations can achieve good results. If for some reason the company does not want to undertake the effort involved in making such a division, a method of ranking the segments relatively is available in the form of the model **Pm-portf.xls,** which consists of three parts: **Market Segm.Char., Product Segm.Char.** and **M_P Portfolio**.

Figure 7.14 shows how Market Segments (MS) and Product Lines (PL) are saved, added and deleted. To add a new MS or PL, press the "add" button. A clean worksheet will then be displayed. To save data for an MS or PL, press the "save" button and type the name of the MS or PL in the pull-down menu. To clean up in the list of MS´s or PL´s, select the MS or PL to delete and press the "delete" button. Then the selected MS or PL will be deleted from the model.

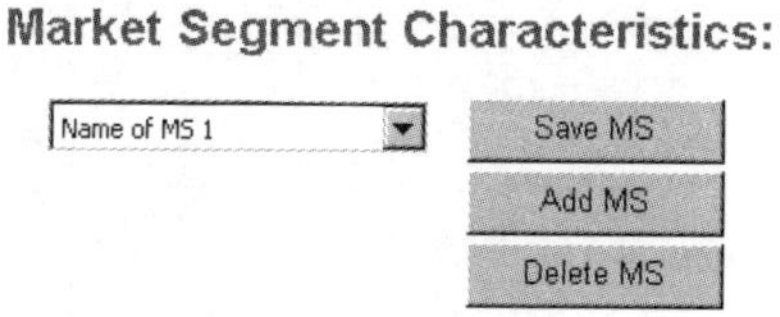

Figure 7.14 – Creating and organising Market Segments. The same applies to Product Lines.

"Market Segment Char." is for ranking customers or customer groups. The ranking is done by giving each factor a weighting according to its importance for the company and evaluating each according to the existing situation as shown in Figure 7.15.

Example of factors:

- If the company's Net Income is relatively high and the Discounts offered are relatively low, Discounts may be of little or no importance; if on the other hand Net Income is relatively low and Discounts very high, then Discounts may be of vital importance.

- If Sales and Marketing expenses are generally low compared to Total Sales, they can be weighted low. If they comprise a larger part of Total Sales, they must be weighted as very important.

- If Customer Loyalty is very high and Price Sensitivity is low, then the Number of Competing Suppliers can be weighted low. If, however, customers very often change suppliers and Price Sensitivity is high, the competition must be weighted correspondingly high.

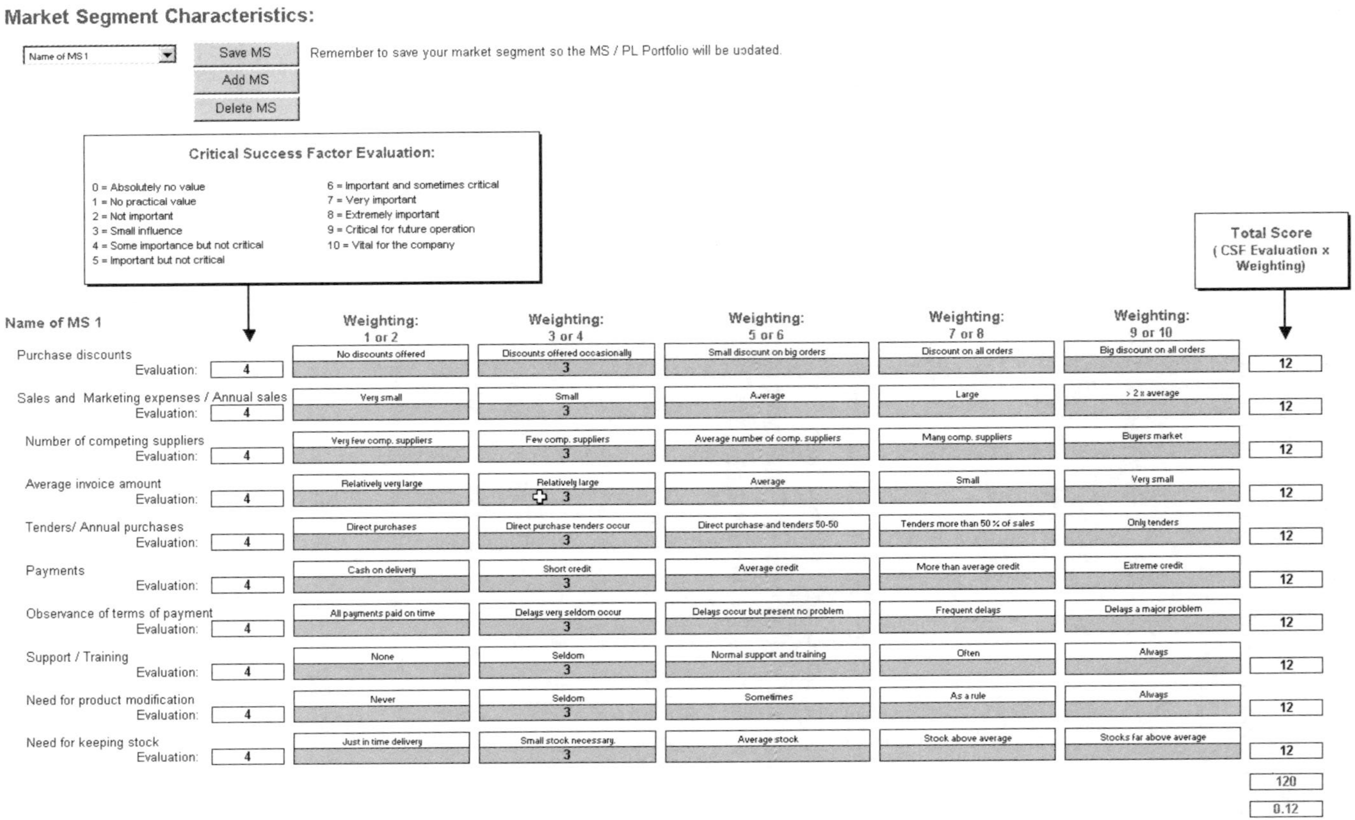

Figure 7.15 – The Market Segments Characteristics Sheet

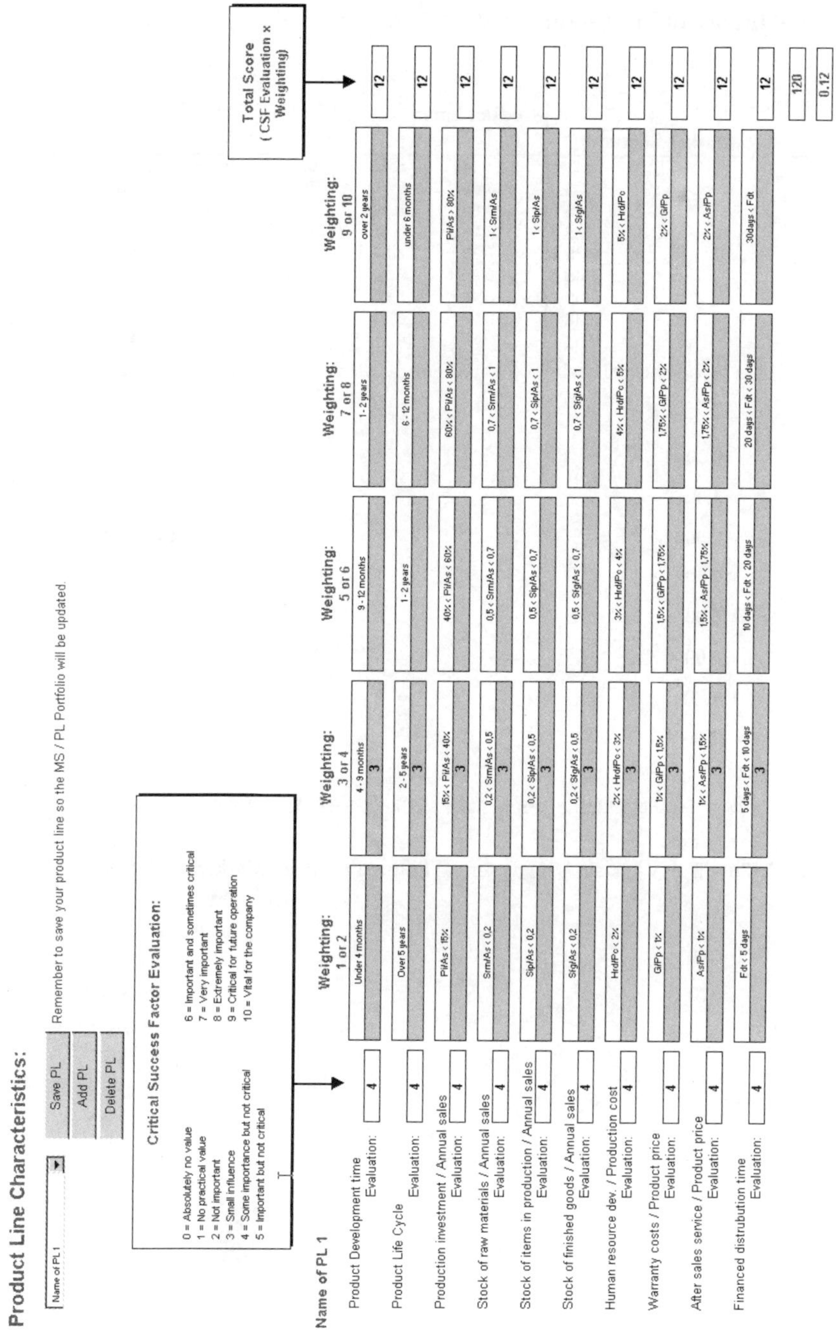

Figure 7.16 – The Product Line Characteristics Sheet

Potential Future Market/ Product Portfolio:

Min value: 4.12

Market Segment:	PL 1	PL 2	PL 3	PL 4	PL 5	Min MS
	Product Line:					
MS 1	14.14	8.46	9.89	10.26	7.63	
MS 2	8.46	5.06	5.92	6.14	4.57	
MS 3	9.89	5.92	6.92	7.18	5.34	
MS 4	10.26	6.14	7.18	7.45	5.54	
MS 5	7.63	4.57	5.34	5.54	4.12	4.12
MS 6	9.89	5.92	6.92	7.18	5.34	
MS 7	8.46	5.06	5.92	6.14	4.57	
MS 8	10.26	6.14	7.18	7.45	5.54	
Min PL					4.12	

Figure 7.17a - The Sheet showing Potential Future Market / Product Portfolios

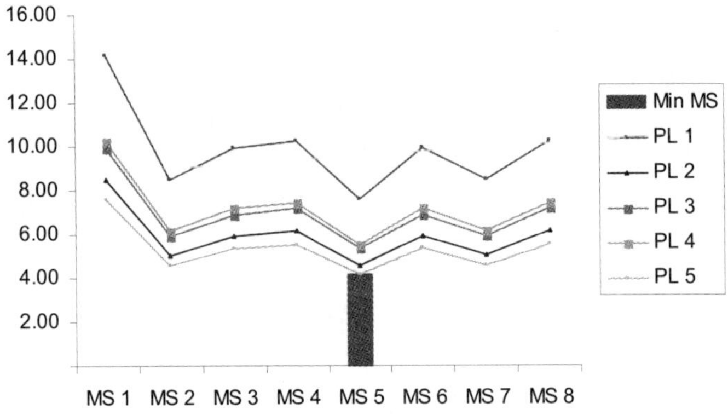

Figure 7.17b - The Graph showing Potential Future Product / Market Portfolios

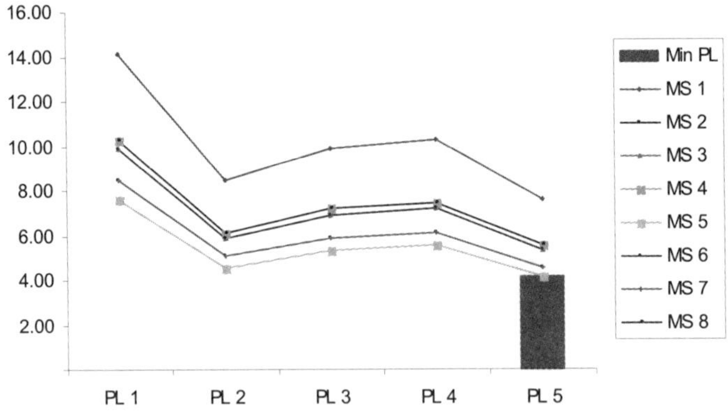

Figure 7.17c - The Graph showing Potential Future Market / Product Portfolios

- If the invoice amount per order is very high or is stipulated via agreement, as e.g. in building construction, then the significance of the Average invoice amount may be small and it can be weighted low. If, on the other hand, the value of one order is small, then the number of invoices per customer becomes more significant and calls for greater weighting of the Average invoice amount.

Each weighting allows a choice of two values e.g. 1 - 2 or 7 –8. The weighting must be made according to which end of the interval is closer to the actual situation.

"Product Segm. Char." is built up in the same way as "Market Segm. Char." (see Figure 7.16) and must be operated in the same way. Small problems can arise because of the situation in a particular industry or branch. In some cases, product development periods can be considerably different from the ones stipulated. In these cases, the user must insert normal conditions for the industry or branch in question, bearing in mind that the evaluations 5 – 6 represent the average.

"PM Portfolio" is calculated by the program and ranks the various segments (see Figure 7.17). The combination of Market Segment and Product or Product Line that produces the lowest score will be the most advantageous as the basis for growth. In the example below, the combination Market Segment 5 and Product 5 is the most advantageous, while the combination Market Segment 1 and Product 1 produces the highest score and should under no circumstances be chosen as the basis for growth efforts.

Potential Future Market/ Product Portfolio:

Min value: 4.12

Market Segment:	Product Line: PL 1	PL 2	PL 3	PL 4	PL 5	Min MS
MS 1	14.14	8.46	9.89	10.26	7.63	
MS 2	8.46	5.06	5.92	6.14	4.57	
MS 3	9.89	5.92	6.92	7.18	5.34	
MS 4	10.26	6.14	7.18	7.45	5.54	
MS 5	7.63	4.57	5.34	5.54	4.12	4.12
MS 6	9.89	5.92	6.92	7.18	5.34	
MS 7	8.46	5.06	5.92	6.14	4.57	
MS 8	10.26	6.14	7.18	7.45	5.54	
Min PL					4.12	

Figure 7.18 - Example 1: values.

The diagram below is the graphic presentation of the values in Figure 7.18, and gives an easier grasp of the mutual relationship between different combinations of market segments and products/product groups.

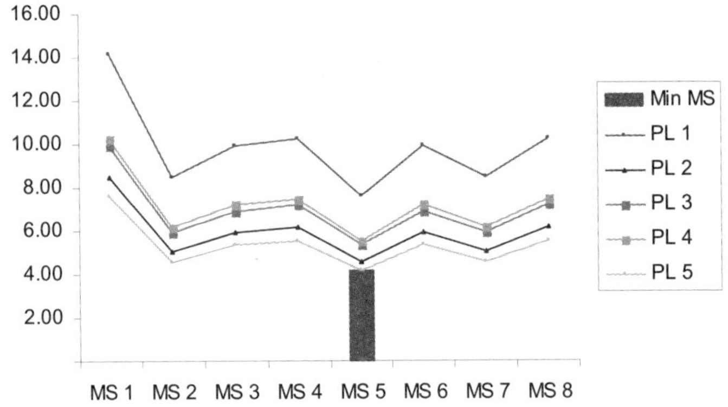

Figure 7.19 - Example 1, graphic presentation.

The example shows that the best basis for expansion will be the combination of Product/Product Line 5 and Market Segment 5.

7.4 Calculation of Company Value

7.4.1 Model: NPV.xls

NPV.xls. consists of two parts: "**NPV static**" and "**NPV dynamic**", plus two corresponding graphs.

"NPV static" operates with fixed Net Profit Rate, Capital Efficiency and Growth Rate.

The Equity Surplus shows the company's ability to make a profit larger than necessary to build up or maintain the set Equity Ratio goal. In other words, if positive, it represents capital that can be used for purposes other than the running and development of the company, e.g. diversification through mergers or acquisitions. If negative, it represents the extra capital that must be invested in the company if the present strategy is to be maintained and Equity Ratio goal is to be achieved.

The program calculates a value of the company consisting of the Net Present Value of a future Equity Surplus plus the Present Equity. It can always be disputed whether this value actually represents the real value of the company. Certainly it seldom represents the actual sales value, which might be either higher or lower, depending upon the number of potential buyers.

Company: **DemoCompany Ltd.**

Amounts in: **1000 GBP**

	Year 0	Year 1	Year 2	Year 3	Year 4	Year 5	Year 6	Year 7	Year 8	Year 9	Year 10
Basic Assumtions:											
Growth Rate (G)	**0.100**										
Return on Sale (ROS)	**0.070**										
Capital Efficiency (CE)	**1.926**										
Calc. Interest rate	**0.080**										
Equity Ratio - Objectives:											
Equity Ratio Objective (ER-Goal)	**0.35**										
Results:											
Sales	**84,110**	92,521	101,773	111,950	123,145	135,460	149,006	163,907	180,297	198,327	218,160
Total assets (Capital) (I)	43,671	48,038	52,842	58,126	63,938	70,332	77,366	85,102	93,612	102,974	113,271
Equity (E)	**13,299.00**	21,172.49	22,700.97	24,382.29	26,231.75	28,266.16	30,504.00	32,965.63	35,673.43	38,652.00	41,928.43
Equity Goal (Eg)	15,284.79	16,813.27	18,494.59	20,344.05	22,378.46	24,616.30	27,077.93	29,785.73	32,764.30	36,040.73	39,644.80
Equity surplus:	-1,985.79	4,359.22	4,206.37	4,038.24	3,853.29	3,649.85	3,426.07	3,179.91	2,909.13	2,611.27	2,283.63
Net Present Value:	-1,985.79	4,036.32	3,606.29	3,205.69	2,832.29	2,484.03	2,159.01	1,855.45	1,571.71	1,306.29	1,057.76

Company Net Present Value:		
Equity surplus NPV (accum. 5 years)	**14,178.82**	
Equity surplus NPV (accum. 10 years)	**22,129.03**	
Company Value - 5 years	**29,463.61**	Equity goal (year 0) + NPV of Equity surplus (accum. 5 years)
Company Value - 10 years	**37,413.81**	Equity goal (year 0) + NPV of Equity surplus (accum. 10 yers)

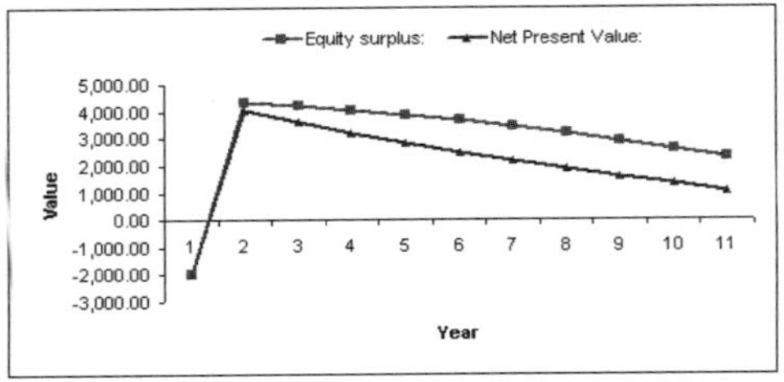

Figure 7.20 – The Net Present Value Static Sheet.

Company: **DemoCompany Ltd.**

Amounts in: **1000 GBP**

	Year 0	Year 1	Year 2	Year 3	Year 4	Year 5	Year 6	Year 7	Year 8	Year 9	Year 10
Basic Assumtions:											
Growth Rate (G)		**0.400**	**0.400**	**0.600**	**0.600**	**0.500**	**0.500**	**0.400**	**0.400**	**0.300**	**0.300**
Return on Sale (ROS)	**0.070**	**0.090**	**0.090**	**0.090**	**0.100**	**0.100**	**0.100**	**0.100**	**0.090**	**0.090**	**0.090**
Capital Efficiency (CE)	**1.926**	**1.744**	**1.607**	**1.499**	**1.413**	**1.343**	**1.285**	**1.237**	**1.196**	**1.161**	**1.200**
Calc. Interest rate	**0.080**										
Equity Ratio - Objectives:											
Equity Ratio Objective (ER-Goal)	**0.35**	**0.35**	**0.35**	**0.35**	**0.35**	**0.35**	**0.35**	**0.35**	**0.35**	**0.35**	**0.35**
Results:											
Annual Sales	**84,110**	117,754	164,856	263,769	422,030	633,046	949,568	1,329,396	1,861,154	2,419,500	3,145,350
Total assets (Capital) (I)	43,671	67,519	102,586	175,963	298,677	471,367	738,964	1,074,693	1,556,149	2,083,979	2,621,125
Equity (E)	**13299.00**	25882.65	38468.83	59644.28	103790.18	167841.43	259935.18	391576.82	543646.48	762407.02	1012474.23
Equity Goal (Eg)	15284.79	23631.82	35905.08	61587.15	104536.88	164978.35	258637.27	376142.64	544652.03	729392.74	917393.72
Equity surplus:	-1985.79	2250.82	2563.75	-1942.86	-746.70	2863.08	1297.91	15434.18	-1005.55	33014.28	95080.51
Net Present Value:	-1985.79	2084.10	2198.00	-1542.31	-548.85	1948.57	817.90	9005.70	-543.27	16515.36	44040.67

Company Net Present Value:		
Equity surplus NPV (accum. 5 years)	**2,153.72**	
Equity surplus NPV (accum. 10 years)	**71,990.09**	
Company Value - 5 years	**17,438.51**	Equity goal (year 0) + NPV of Equity surplus (accum. 5 years)
Company Value - 10 years	**87,274.88**	Equity goal (year 0) + NPV of Equity surplus (accum. 10 yers)

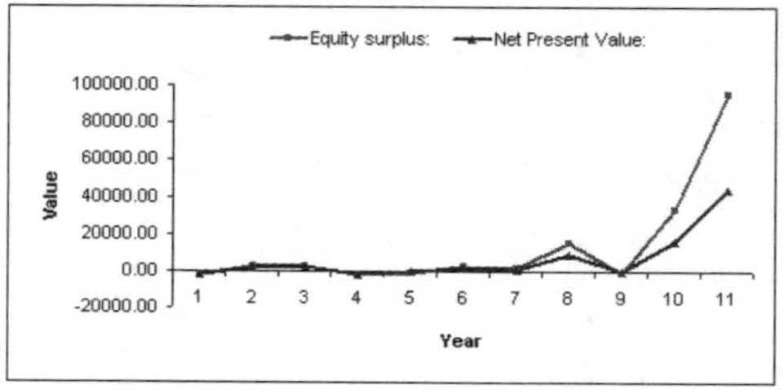

Figure 7.21 – The Net Present Value Dynamic Sheet

The philosophy behind the calculation is that a part of the profit made must be reinvested in simply maintaining the company and therefore represents little or no value to the present owners. If, therefore, the company could be sold at a price higher than, e.g., its value based upon the Equity Surplus accumulated over 5 or 10 years plus its Present Equity, it would be more advantageous for the owner to sell. Likewise if the Company Value forecast after 10 years is lower than that after 5 years, it will be appropriate to sell. If on the contrary the value of the company is increasing considerately and to more than a possible sales price over a period of 5 or 10 years, it might be advantageous to keep it. At the same time, the calculated value can be a guideline for fixing a possible price for sales negotiations. Any price below the value forecast in 5 years' time would be unacceptable, while a price between the values forecast in 5 and 10 years' time might be worth considering.

The NPV-SD dynamic model operates in exactly the same way as the static part, with the only difference that the user can insert any value for the Net Profit Rate, Capital Efficiency and Growth Rate. Therefore, values for each year must be inserted individually, and similarly the Equity Ratio Goal can be altered all through the period.

7.5 Calculation of Trends and Capital Efficiency

7.5.1 Model: Calc-Sbudget.xls

Calc-Sbudget.xls. consists of two models "**U-values**" and "**Correlation Calc.**" plus two graphs.

These two programs are tools for analysing the denominators in the ER_n equation, Growth rate, Net Profit Rate and Capital Efficiency.

U-values

The U-values model presents a short cut for calculating Capital Efficiency providing that Fixed Assets are divided between relevant customer groups according to their share of Total Sales, an approximation which is not correct but is sufficiently accurate for practical purposes. The philosophy behind the model is as follows.

If the initial input in a period "n" results in sales of, e.g., $1 and 80% of the customers pay for their purchase in period "n+1", then only 80% of turnover can be recycled into costs and stocks in this period, unless resources are brought in from other funds. If 20% of the customers pay for their purchases in period "n+2", then 20% of the initial input plus 80% of the input from period "n+1" can be recycled. That means that unless resources are supplied from other funds, the total turnover is limited by the input in costs and stocks and the speed with which purchases are converted to cash for the company. The U-values indicate the described recycling process depending upon the percentage of purchases paid for in the periods following the sales.

For example, if, as in the table below, 80% of the purchases from period "n" are converted into cash in the period "n+1" and 20% in the period "n+2", then the U-value will be 0.8333

Period	n	n+1	n+2	n+3	n+4	n+5	n+6	n+7	n+8
% liquidity return	1.0000	0.8000	0.2000						

Figure 7.22 – Example of purchases turned into cash in two periods.

If the payments are distributed differently, e.g. as in Figure 7.23, the U-value will be 0.4762

Period	n	n+1	n+2	n+3	n+4	n+5	n+6	n+7	n+8
% liquidity return	1.0000	0.4000	0.3000	0.1500	0.1000	0.0500			

Figure 7.23 – Example of purchases converted into cash in five periods.

Company: **Company X Ltd.**
Year:
Amounts in: **GBP**

Calculation of "U-values"

Period	n	n+1	n+2	n+3	n+4	n+5	n+6	n+7	n+8	n+9	n+10	n+11	n+12	n+13	n+14	n+15	n+16	n+17	n+18	n+19	n+20
% liquidity return	**1.0000**	0.8000	0.2000																		
Operational costs																					
liquidity return	1.0000	0.8000	0.2000	0.0000	0.0000	0.0000	0.0000	0.0000	0.0000	0.0000	0.0000	0.0000	0.0000	0.0000	0.0000	0.0000	0.0000	0.0000	0.0000	0.0000	0.0000
liquidity return n+1	0.8000		0.6400	0.1600	0.0000	0.0000	0.0000	0.0000	0.0000	0.0000	0.0000	0.0000	0.0000	0.0000	0.0000	0.0000	0.0000	0.0000	0.0000	0.0000	0.0000
liquidity return n+2	0.8400			0.6720	0.1680	0.0000	0.0000	0.0000	0.0000	0.0000	0.0000	0.0000	0.0000	0.0000	0.0000	0.0000	0.0000	0.0000	0.0000	0.0000	0.0000
liquidity return n+3	0.8320				0.6656	0.1664	0.0000	0.0000	0.0000	0.0000	0.0000	0.0000	0.0000	0.0000	0.0000	0.0000	0.0000	0.0000	0.0000	0.0000	0.0000
liquidity return n+4	0.8336					0.6669	0.1667	0.0000	0.0000	0.0000	0.0000	0.0000	0.0000	0.0000	0.0000	0.0000	0.0000	0.0000	0.0000	0.0000	0.0000
liquidity return n+5	0.8333						0.6666	0.1667	0.0000	0.0000	0.0000	0.0000	0.0000	0.0000	0.0000	0.0000	0.0000	0.0000	0.0000	0.0000	0.0000
liquidity return n+6	0.8333							0.6667	0.1667	0.0000	0.0000	0.0000	0.0000	0.0000	0.0000	0.0000	0.0000	0.0000	0.0000	0.0000	0.0000
liquidity return n+7	0.8333								0.6667	0.1667	0.0000	0.0000	0.0000	0.0000	0.0000	0.0000	0.0000	0.0000	0.0000	0.0000	0.0000
liquidity return n+8	0.8333									0.6667	0.1667	0.0000	0.0000	0.0000	0.0000	0.0000	0.0000	0.0000	0.0000	0.0000	0.0000
liquidity return n+9	0.8333										0.6667	0.1667	0.0000	0.0000	0.0000	0.0000	0.0000	0.0000	0.0000	0.0000	0.0000
liquidity return n+10	0.8333											0.6667	0.1667	0.0000	0.0000	0.0000	0.0000	0.0000	0.0000	0.0000	0.0000
liquidity return n+11	0.8333												0.6667	0.1667	0.0000	0.0000	0.0000	0.0000	0.0000	0.0000	0.0000
liquidity return n+12	0.8333													0.6667	0.1667	0.0000	0.0000	0.0000	0.0000	0.0000	0.0000
liquidity return n+13	0.8333														0.6667	0.1667	0.0000	0.0000	0.0000	0.0000	0.0000
liquidity return n+14	0.8333															0.6667	0.1667	0.0000	0.0000	0.0000	0.0000
liquidity return n+15	0.8333																0.6667	0.1667	0.0000	0.0000	0.0000
liquidity return n+16	0.8333																	0.6667	0.1667	0.0000	0.0000
liquidity return n+17	0.8333																		0.6667	0.1667	0.0000
liquidity return n+18	0.8333																			0.6667	0.1667
liquidity return n+19	0.8333																				0.6667
liquidity return n+20	0.8333																				

U-values	**0.8333**
Gross Profit Ratio	**0.0700**
Net Profit Ratio	**0.0270**
Total sales	**84,110**
Total fixed assets	**21,837**
Capital Efficiency	**0.7102**

Formula for Capital efficiency:

$$\frac{\text{U-values}}{(1 - \text{Gross Profit Ratio} + \text{Net Profit Ratio}) + ((\text{Total assets} / \text{Total sales}) * \text{U-values})}$$

Figure 7.24 – The U-Values Sheet (Calculation of Capital Efficiency)

Number of years: 4

Assumptions:	Year 1996	% of sales	Year 1997	% of sales	Year 1998	% of sales	Budget 1999	% of sales	Average	% of sales
Sales	100		110		155		175		135	
Net Profit	10	10%	12	11%	25	16%	29	17%	19	14%

Correlation for Net Profit Rate:

	x	y	xy	x^2	
	1	0.1000	0.1000	1	
	2	0.1091	0.2182	4	
	3	0.1613	0.4839	9	
	4	0.1657	0.6629	16	
	10	0.5361	1.4649	30	
Gradient:		0.0249	Average:		0.1340
Start v:y		0.0717			

Line	Net Profit Rate	Avg
0	0.0717	0.1340
1	0.0966	0.1340
2	0.1216	0.1340
3	0.1465	0.1340
4	0.1714	0.1340
5	0.1964	0.1340
6	0.2213	0.1340
7	0.2462	0.1340
8	0.2712	0.1340
9	0.2961	0.1340
10	0.3210	0.1340

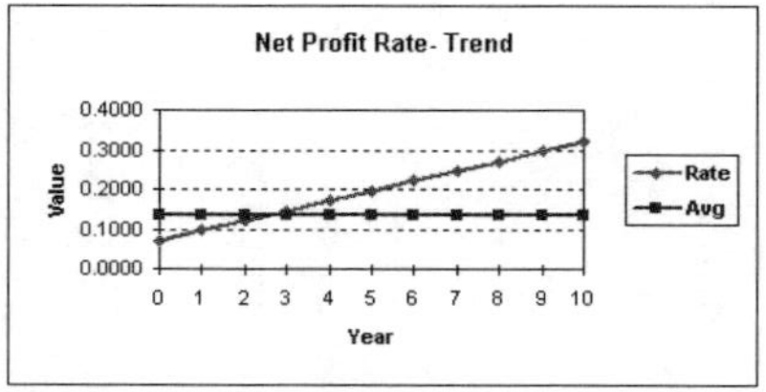

Correlation for Growth rate:

	x	y	xy	x^2	
	1	0.1000	0.1000	1	
	2	0.4091	0.8182	4	
	3	0.1290	0.3871	9	
	6	0.6381	1.3053	14	
Gradient:		0.0338	Average G:		0.1674
Start v:y		0.1450		175	175

Line	Growth rate	Avg
0	0.1450	0.1674
1	0.1789	0.1674
2	0.2127	0.1674
3	0.2465	0.1674
4	0.2804	0.1674
5	0.3142	0.1674
6	0.3481	0.1674
7	0.3819	0.1674
8	0.4157	0.1674
9	0.4496	0.1674
10	0.4834	0.1674

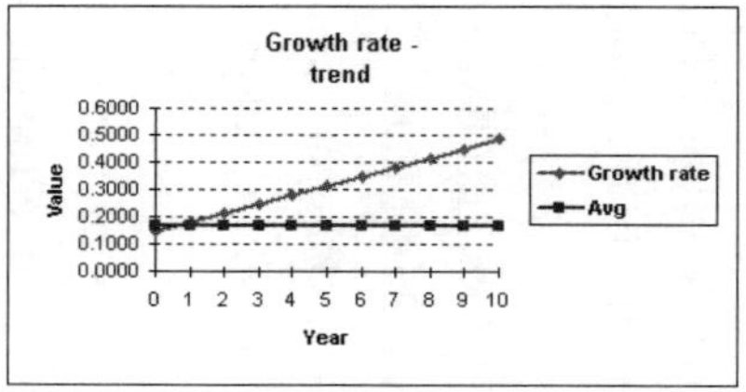

Figure 7.25 – The Correlation Calc. Sheet

Calculating Capital Efficiency from U-values requires the following values to be inserted in the program:

- GNPRs Profit Rate
- Net Profit Rate
- Total Sales of the company
- Total Fixed Assets of the company

On the basis of the values thus inserted, the program will calculate and indicate a value for Capital Efficiency. Again, it must be realised that the calculated Capital Efficiency is not correct because it is based upon the assumption that any segment requires investments in Fixed Assets proportional to its share of Total Sales, which in many cases is absolutely not correct. For practical purposes, however this approximation is quite sufficient.

It is important to notice that Sales follow immediately after production in the two tables. If goods have to be delayed in stock for e.g. 1 period as shown in the table below, the U-value will be reduced to 0.3226 and Capital Efficiency reduced correspondingly:

Period	n	n+1	n+2	n+3	n+4	n+5	n+6	n+7	n+8
% liquidity return	1.0000		0.4000	0.3000	0.1500	0.1000	0.0500		

Figure 7.26 – Example of a one-period delay in the conversion of purchases into cash.

Given that production for a certain customer or customer group takes 1 period and production costs are 200,000, goods produced remain 1 period in stock before being delivered, 80% of customers pay 1 period after delivery and 20% 2 periods after delivery, market contribution for the product is 40% and the company's Net Profit Rate is 2%, the company's Total Sales (including all customers and products) are 9,000,000 and Total Fixed Assets are 1,000,000, then the following values are inserted in the program:

Period	n	n+1	n+2	n+3	n+4	n+5	n+6	n+7	n+8
% liquidity return	1.0000		0.8000	0.2000					

Figure 7.27 - Example.

This results in a U-value of	0.4556
GNPRs profit rate (contribution margin):	0.40
Net Profit Rate	0.02
Company's Total Sales	9,000,000
Company's Total Assets	1,000,000
Which result in a Capital Efficiency of	0.679

Correlation calculation

The Correlation calculation model consists of three parts: the Correlation calculation model and two graphs: the NPR-Trend Graph and the Growth rate-Trend Graph.

The Correlation calculation model calculates an average for Net Profit Rate and Growth Rate based, respectively, on the net profit rates and growth rates from the profit and loss accounts for the number of years inserted in the program; the average rates are used to forecast the company's prospects. However, it must be realised that using averages for simulations presupposes a very stable company and environment. Nevertheless it gives a picture of the company's future if no significant changes take place.

Furthermore the program calculates a linear trend by linear correlation, which indicates the development of the Net Profit Rate and Growth Rate from which values can be extracted for use in simulations. In using the trends it must be realised that a single "good" or "bad" year will either increase or reduce the gradient of the linear correlation, just as linear trends will always end up in unrealistic figures. Trends must therefore always be used with care.

Appendix A
Installation and setup guide

Macintosh:

Basic requirements:

- A Macintosh compatible computer, OS version 6.7 or later.
- 4 MB RAM or more.
- 6 MB or more free hard disc space, 4 MB for basic data files and 2 MB for working data files for each company.
- MS Excel version 5.0 or Excel 98 for Macintosh.

Installation:

1. Create a new folder on your computer to keep the basic data files and the company's working models. The user determines where the models are to be stored in the computer, but we recommend naming the new folder "Strategic Budgeting".
2. Insert the CD disc in the CD-drive of your computer.
3. Open the CD disc.
4. Open the "Macintosh" folder on the CD.
5. Open the appropriate Excel folder on the CD:
   - Open the "Excel 5" folder if you are running Excel 5
   - Open the "Excel 98" folder if you are running Excel 98.
6. Copy the "Base" and "Demo" folders in their entirety into your newly created folder.

Windows:

Basic requirements:

- A Windows 95/98/NT 4.0 operating system compatible computer.
- 4 MB RAM (or more, depending on the operating system).
- 6 MB or more free hard disc space, 4 MB for basic data files and 2 MB for working data files for each company.
- MS Excel version 5.0, Excel 95, Excel 97 or Excel 2000.

Installation:

1. Insert the CD disc in the CD-drive of your computer.
2. Open the CD disc through "My Computer" or by running Windows Explorer.
3. Double click the "Setup.exe" program on the CD.
4. The setup wizard will guide you through the setup process in 6 steps.

Step 1: The Strategic Budgeting setup Welcome screen.

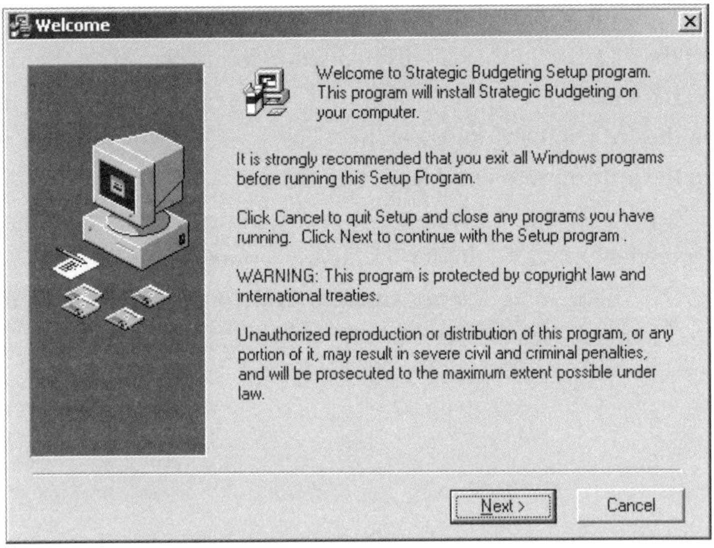

Fig. 1 – Step one is the Welcome screen. Press Next to continue

If you have other Windows programs still running then it is recommended to close them all before continuing to install Strategic Budgeting. Press the Next button to continue.

Step 2: Strategic Budgeting setup requires that you agree to the terms of the License Agreement.

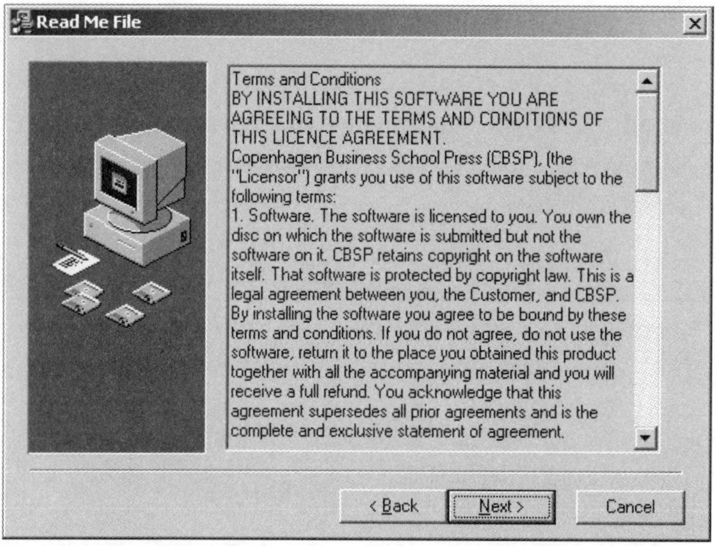

Fig. 2 – Accepting the terms of the software License Agreement.

Press Next if you accept the terms; otherwise press Cancel. If you press Cancel the setup process will be cancelled.

Step 3: Selecting a destination folder for the Strategic Budgeting files.

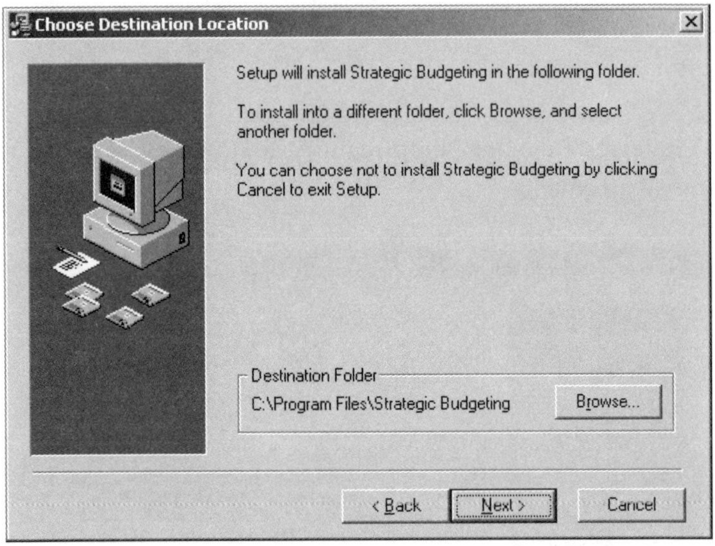

Fig. 3 - Step three for selection of a destination folder. Press Next to continue

The default destination folder is the Windows Program Files folder. As the Strategic Budgeting program consists of Excel files only, you might want to change the destination folder to the same folder as you store other Excel files in, i.e. a standard Windows "My document" folder. Press the "Browse" button if you want to change the destination folder. Press the Next button to continue.

Step 4: Select the components of Strategic Budgeting you want to install.

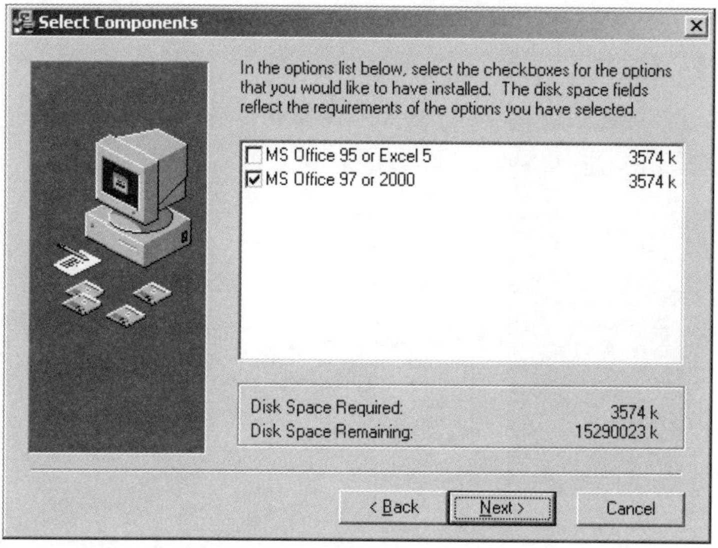

Fig. 4 – Step four allows selection of versions for MS Office 95 or Office 97. Press Next to continue.

Select only one of the components. If you select both components, versions for both MS Office 95 and MS Office 2000 will be installed. Press the Next button to continue.

Step 5: Select a name for the program folder, which will be displayed in the Programs folder which is opened through the Windows Start button.

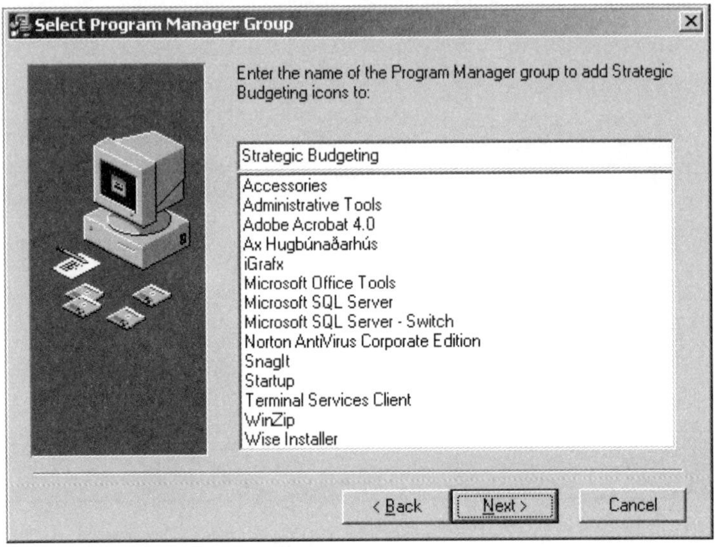

Fig. 5 - Step five allows selection of the program folder. Press Next to continue

The Strategic Budgeting setup will create a program folder with a shortcut to the Strategic Budgeting "New-Comp" Excel program. The shortcut will be placed in the Windows Programs folder.

Step 6: You have now completed the installation of Strategic Budgeting Excel sheets.

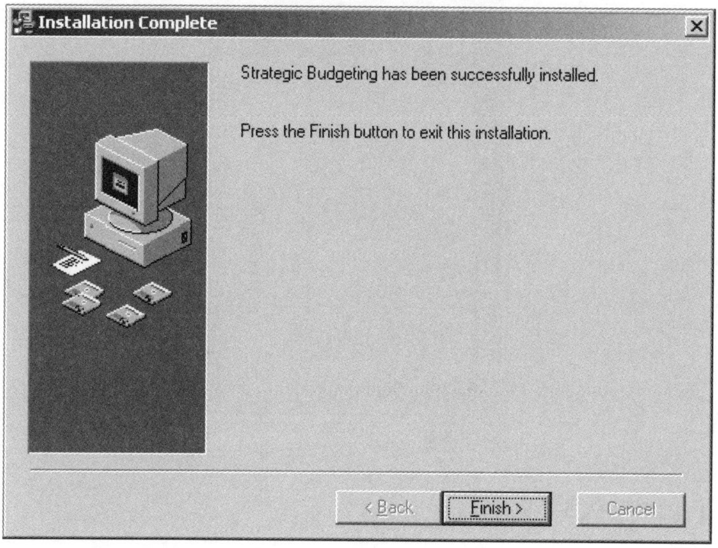

Fig. 6 – Step six, finishing setup. Press Finish to continue

Press Finish to complete the installation. If any errors occur, you must restart the setup.exe program from the CD.

Creating a new company

To start using the Strategic Budgeting models, a new company must be created. A shortcut for creating a new company can be found under "Strategic Budgeting" under "Programs" under the Windows "Start" button.

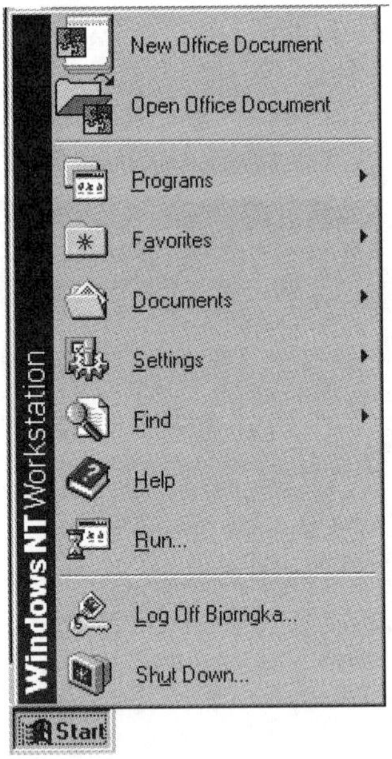

Fig. 7 – The Windows Start menu

From the "Strategic Budgeting" menu, select "Create New Company". This will open the "New_Comp.xls" document. The document will guide you through creating working documents for a new company.

Fig. 8 – Shortcut for creating a new company.

Excel virus warning dialog

As many of the documents contain programs, you may be warned by the Excels virus warning dialog.

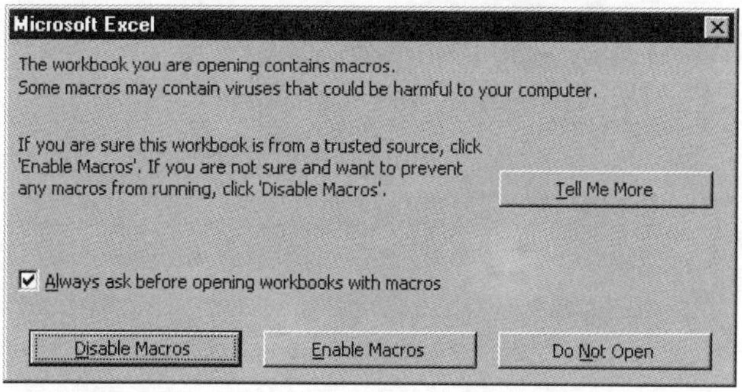

Fig. 9 – The Microsoft Excel virus warning dialog.

The original documents have been tested against viruses, so you can safely select "Enable Macros". If you are still sceptical, you can select "Disable Macros", but then some documents may lose some of their functionality.

If you choose to continue with "New_Comp.xls", you will be prompted with the start-up form.

Fig. 10 – The start-up form of the model.

Choose "Continue" to move to the menu for company registration.

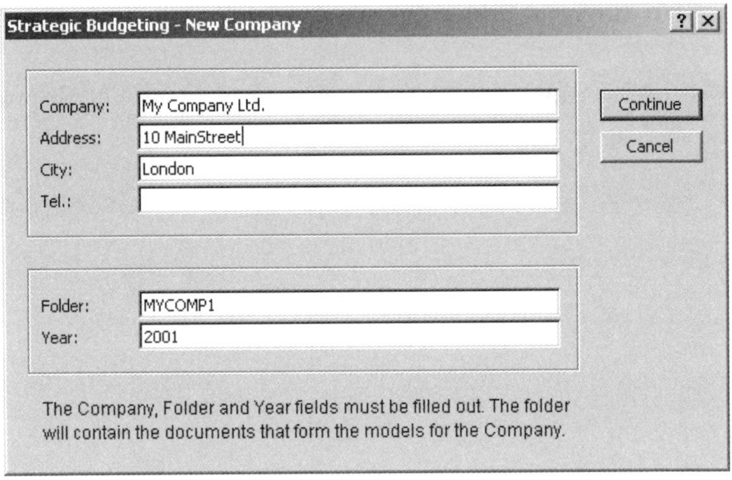

Fig. 11 - Menu for company registration.

Data about the company is entered by overwriting the existing text. The name of the company, its folder and the year to be analysed must be entered in the menu. The folder name refers to the folder in which the company's models (documents) are stored. The year entered in "Year" will be the name of the folder where the models (documents) for that operational year are stored. The year is also recorded automatically in the documents.

Select "Create" to confirm the creation of the company records. The model will then create all the working documents and place them in the appropriate folder. Fig. 12 shows how the working documents for each company are stored in the computer's folder structure.

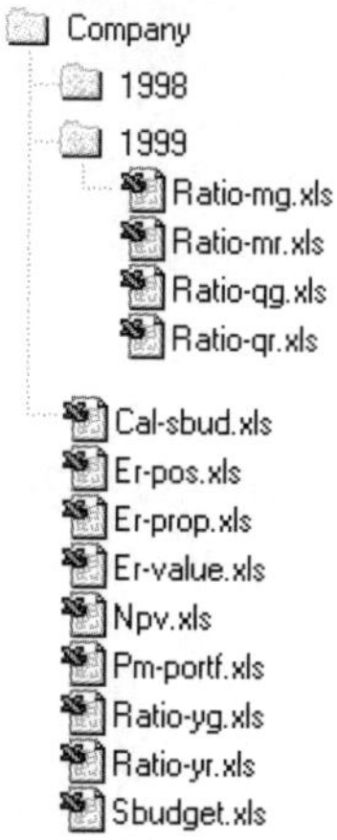

Fig. 12 - The company's folder structure.

As can be seen from Fig. 12, there are four working documents in the folder "1999". These are documents for operational ratio analysis by quarters and months. The folder "Company" contains two working documents for operational ratio analysis for comparison of one year to the next and seven working documents for strategic ratio analysis.

When documents have been created for the company, the model will confirm that the installation is complete and give the user the opportunity of choosing a document to open.

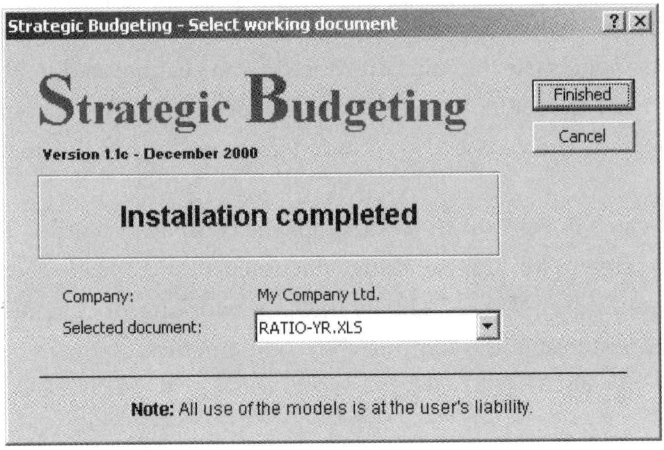

Fig. 13 - Installation of documents completed.

Location of documents

From the "Strategic Budgeting" menu, select "Strategic budgeting files". This will open a folder containing all documents created by the installation process.

Fig. 14 – Selecting the location of installed documents.

Warning

If the name of a document is changed, some of the models will not work properly.

NB: THE NAMES OF DOCUMENTS MAY NOT BE CHANGED.

Cal-Sbud.xls
Er-pos.xls
Er-prop.xls
Er-value.xls
NEW-COMP.xls
NPV.xls
PM-portf.xls
RATIO-MG.xls
RATIO-MR.xls
RATIO-QG.xls
RATIO-QR.xls
RATIO-YG.xls
RATIO-YR.xls
Sbudget.xls

Fig. 14 - List of document names that may not be changed.

Printing

All documents in the model are default set for optimised printing on A4 paper. To print worksheets, press the "Print" button on the Excel toolbar or select "Print" from the File menu. If the original settings are altered, they will be stored with the document.

TIP Several worksheets may be printed at the same time by selecting the sheets while holding down the CTRL (Control) button. Then all the selected sheets will be printed.

Appendix B
Graph Layouts and Customised Ratios

Changes to the layout of the standard graphs

The "GraphData" worksheet contains specifications for all the standard graphs. These specifications determine the appearance and properties of the graphs. Users may change the following standard properties of the graphs (see Figs. 1 and 2):

- The title.
- The legend of the Y-axis,
  - the amount (e.g. GBP or GBP '000s),
  - the ratio.
- The legend of the X-axis.
- The description of the paths.
- The type:
  - Line
  - Bar
  - Pie
- Name of the worksheet where the graph is stored.

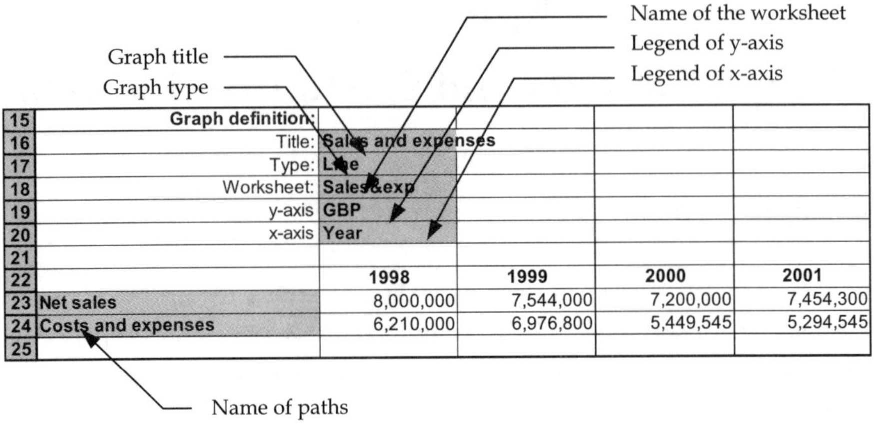

15	Graph definition:				
16	Title:	Sales and expenses			
17	Type:	Line			
18	Worksheet:	Sales&exp			
19	y-axis	GBP			
20	x-axis	Year			
21					
22		1998	1999	2000	2001
23	Net sales	8,000,000	7,544,000	7,200,000	7,454,300
24	Costs and expenses	6,210,000	6,976,800	5,449,545	5,294,545
25					

Fig. 1 - Cells which can be changed in order to change the appearance of the graphs.

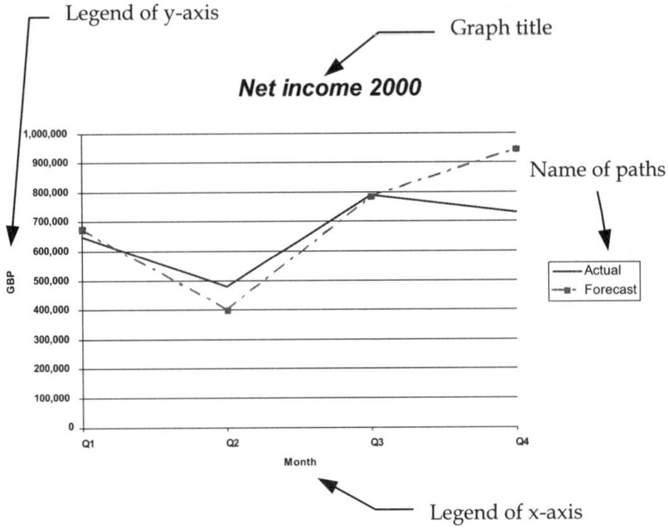

Fig. 2 - Position of the texts which can be changed in the specifications of the graph.

Titles of graphs

Graph titles are a combination of the title shown above and the appropriate operational period. The title should be selected so as to produce the clearest possible description of the contents of the graph (notice that the year is added automatically after the title when the graph is drawn). The year(s) are taken from the "Statements" worksheet in the data documents.

Legend of the Y-axis

The legend of the Y-axis is either retrieved from cell B2 on the "Statements" worksheet, or is entered directly in the "GraphData" worksheet.

Permitted values are as follows:

- Ratio
  (for graphs which display ratios between two quantities).
- B2
  (A formula which retrieves data from cell B2 at the top of the "GraphData" worksheet).

Name of paths

The name of each function displayed in the graphs is entered here.

Type of graphs

The permitted values are:

- Line.
- Bar.
- Pie.

Name of the worksheet where the graph is stored

The following must be borne in mind when choosing the names of the worksheets which contain graphs:

- No two worksheets may have the same name.
- Long names should not be chosen, and abbreviations should be avoided, even though they are permissible.

TIP The "Y-axis" cell contains the currency unit in which data are recorded (e.g. GBP or GBP '000s). The cell is connected to the "Statements" worksheet. If the graph is used to calculate ratios, the text "Ratio" must be entered in the cell. When that is done, all numerical values on the Y-axis will be set up for ratios (to 2 decimal places).

Developing customised ratios

The worksheets for User Ratios are almost the same in all three basic documents (RATIO-YR, RATIO-QR and RATIO-MR). The diagrams in this chapter are based on a quarterly analysis.

Fig. 3 shows the User Ratios worksheet. Users who are not familiar with MS Excel are advised to learn to use that program before developing their own ratios.

The worksheet is divided into 3 units:

- Explanations of the ratios.
- Ratios based on Balance Sheet figures.
- Ratios based on Income Statement and Balance Sheet figures.

1. Number of Employees: **Formula:** Number of employees **Indication:** Average number of employees in the company over the period	**Ratio 3:** **Formula:** __________ **Indication:**	**Ratio 5:** **Formula:** __________ **Indication:**
2. Turnover per Employee: **Formula:** Net sales / Number of employees **Indication:** Average turnover per employee of the company	**Ratio 4:** **Formula:** __________ **Indication:**	**Ratio 6:** **Formula:** __________ **Indication:**

	31 Dec. '99	31 Mar. '00	30 Jun. '00	30 Sep. '00	31 Dec. '00
Ratio 4:					
Ratio 5:					
Ratio 6:					

	Q1		Q2		6 months		Q3		9 months		Q4	
	Actual	Forecast	**Actual**	Forecast	**Actual**	Forecast	**Actual**	Forecast	**Actual**	Forecast	**Actual**	Forecast
1. Number of Employees:					**Average**	Average			**Average**	Average		
Period of operation:												
On an annual basis:												
2. Turnover per Employee:					**Total**	Total			**Total**	Total		
Period of operation:												
On an annual basis:												
Ratio 3:												
Period of operation:												
On an annual basis:												

Fig. 3 - The data entry sheet for User Ratios.

Explanations of the ratios

Explanations of the ratios are to be found at the top of each worksheet. The user enters a description of the ratio (i.e. its name), the formula and what it indicates.

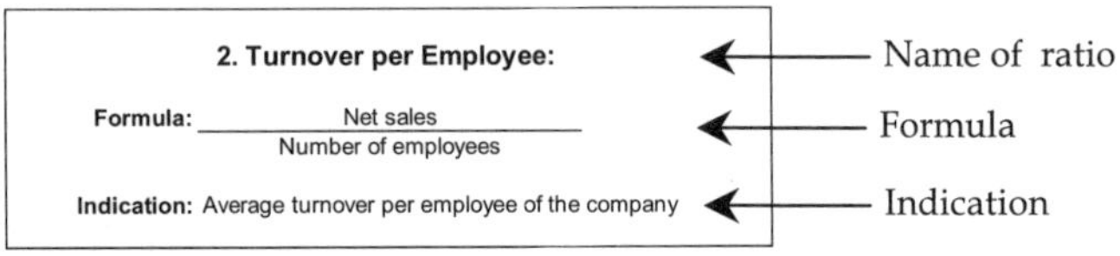

Fig. 4 - How the definition of a ratio is entered.

Ratios based on Balance Sheet figures

These ratios are based on figures from the Balance Sheet only, and not from the Income Statement.

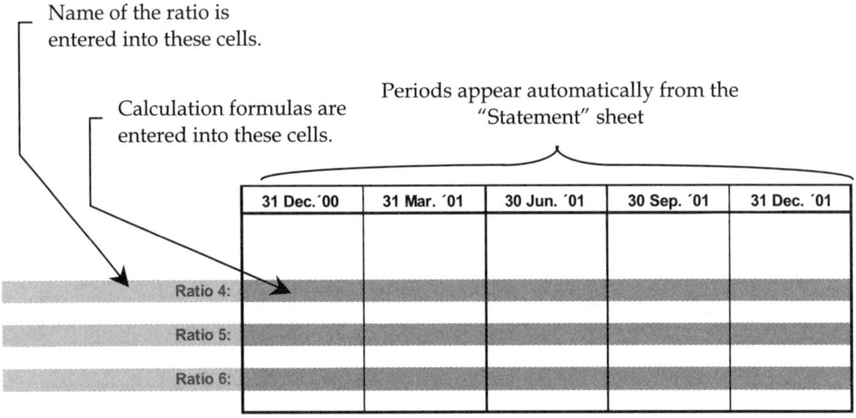

Fig. 5 - The grey areas are cells for the entry of data for calculating Balance Sheet ratios.

Ratios based on Income Statement and Balance Sheet figures

Ratios based on Income Statement and Balance Sheet figures use either figures from the Income Statement or a mixture of Income Statement and Balance Sheet figures.

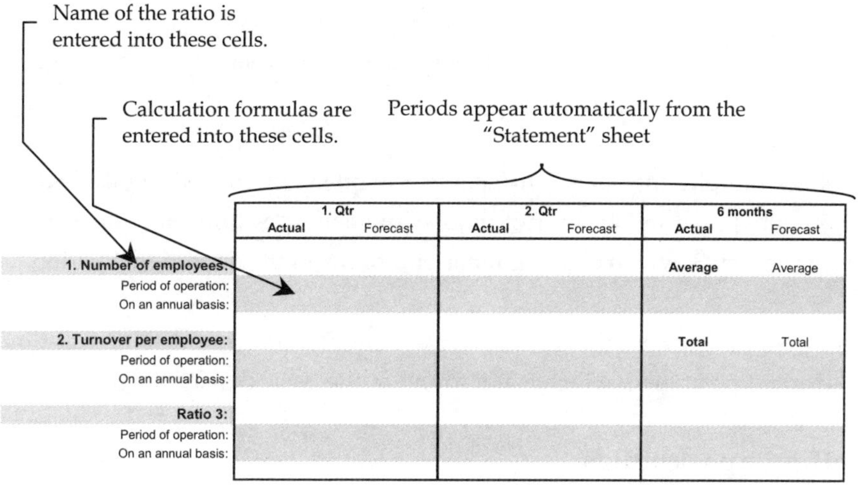

Fig. 6 - The grey areas are cells for the entry of data for calculating Income Statement and Balance Sheet ratios.

When making calculations involving a mixture of figures, i.e. when a figure from the Income Statement is divided into, or by, a figure from the Balance Sheet, it must be borne in mind that the figures must be expressed on an annualised basis. The general rules for doing this are as follows:

- Income Statement figures x 12 months
- Balance Sheet figures or quantity figures x the length of the period in months.

Example 1 - Turnover per employee during the first quarter (Q1):

Operational period: $\dfrac{\text{Sales}}{\text{Full-time equivalent positions}}$

Annualised: $\dfrac{\text{Sales for the period x 12}}{\text{Full-time equivalent positions x 3}}$

In this example, the sales (an Income Statement figure) are multiplied by 12, while the number of full-time equivalent positions (a quantity) is multiplied by 3, which is the number of months in the operational period.

The denominator in the formula is a quantity (the number of full-time equivalent positions), which is not found in the basic data of the model.

Setting up formulas

Setting up formulas makes demands both on the operator's knowledge of how to use the MS Excel program and also his skills in selecting useful scales of measurement.

The following checklist will be of assistance in setting up formulas:

1. Write the name and formula for the ratio on a piece of paper, e.g.

Turnover per employee

Operational period: $\dfrac{\text{Sales}}{\text{Number of full-time equivalent positions}}$

Annualised: $\dfrac{\text{Sales x 12}}{\text{Number of full-time equivalent positions x length (in months)}}$

2. Find the cells on the "Statements" worksheet which contain the values used in the formula and make a note of them, e.g.

   - Cell for sales for Q1 = B9
   - Cell for sales for Q2 = D9
   - Cell for sales for 6 months = F9

   There is no cell for the number of employees; instead, the number of employees for each period may be written directly in the MS Excel formula (see example below).

3. If a ratio is based on Balance Sheet figures only, it is placed in the Balance Sheet ratios; otherwise, it is placed in the Income Statement and Balance Sheet ratios. Enter the name of the ratio in the appropriate place, e.g.:

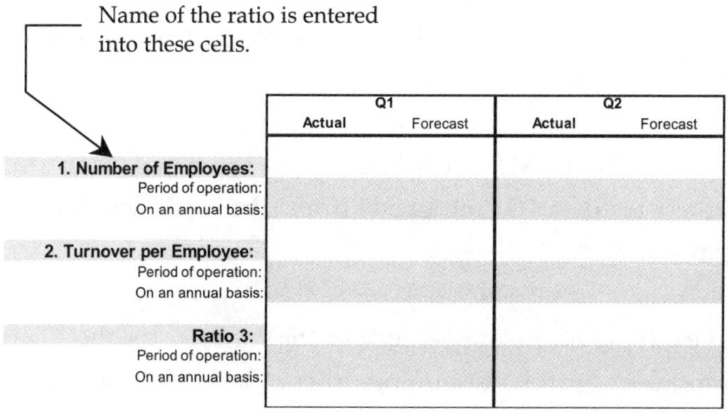

Fig. 7 - The light grey area shows the cell for entering the name of the ratio.

4. Record the formula for the ratio in the appropriate cell, e.g.:

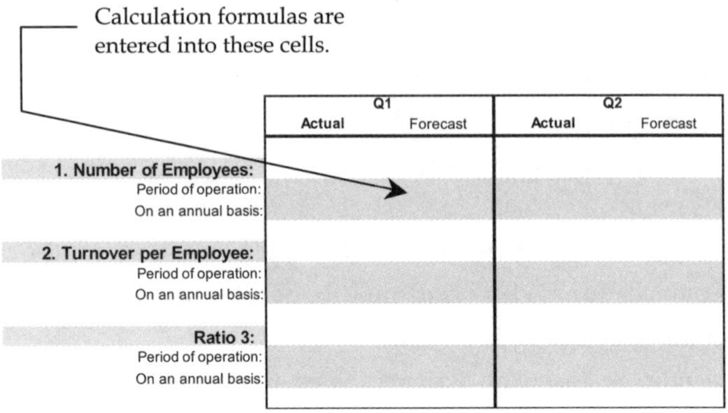

Fig. 8 - The dark grey area shows the cells for entering formulas.

Note that the formula for the ratio must be entered for all the periods to be calculated, i.e. both for the actual figures and forecast for each quarter and for each month.

All formulas in MS Excel begin with the equals sign (=); then the numerical data is retrieved from the cells on the Statements worksheet.

An example of the appearance of the formula for the "Turnover per Employee" ratio (assuming there are 55 full-time-equivalent positions) would be as follows:

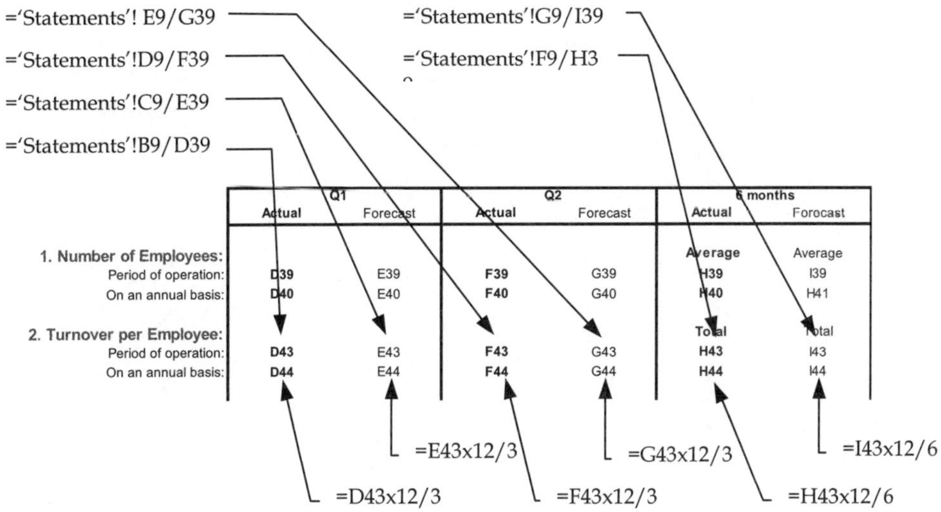

Fig. 9 - An example of the appearance of the formula for the "Turnover per Employee" formulas (based on 55 employees). The formulas are shown both for calculations for an operational period and on an annualised basis. Note that the formulas for the annualised basis are calculated directly on the basis of the cells containing the formulas for the operational periods.

5. The ratio is now a standard part of the model and will be recalculated after every change that is made to the Income Statement and Balance Sheet data.

   If there is a change in the number of full-time equivalent positions, the appropriate changes will have to be made to the formula.

TIP Frequently used numerical values can be recorded in particular cells on the worksheet and then these cells can be referred to in the formula. If the values in the cells are changed, the formula will be recalculated on the basis of the new values.

Definitions

CE	Capital Efficiency
CEn	Capital Efficiency at a given time
EPS	Earnings Per Share
ER budget	The ER budget value is the calculation of the actual Equity Ratio for future periods.
ER goal	Target value of the Equity Ratio.
ER limit	Equity ratio limit is the value that the present actual ER will converge to.
ER	Equity Ratio
ER_g	Target value of the Equity Ratio.
ER_n	Equity ratio limit is the value that the present actual ER will converge to.
G	Growth rate
GNPRs profit rate	Contribution margin
MR	Monthly Ratios
MS	Market Segments
NPR	Net Profit Rate. (The profit figure which is reinvested, i.e. remains in the company).
NPV	Net Present Value
PL	Product Line
QR	Quarterly Ratios
ROA	Return on Total Assets
ROE	Return on Equity
ROI	Return on total Investments
ROS	Return on Sales
YR	Annual (Yearly) Ratios

Models for Strategic Ratio Analysis

Calc-Sbud	Calculation for strategic budgeting
ER- Pos	Equity Ratio Position
ER- Prop	Equity Ratio Proposition

ER- Value	Equity Ratio Value
NPV	Net Present Value
PM- Portfolio	Product and Market Portfolio
Sbudget	Strategic budget

Models for Operational Ratio Analysis

Ratio-mg	Graphs for monthly ratio analysis
Ratio-mr	Ratios for monthly analysis
Ratio-qg	Graphs for quarterly ratio analysis
Ratio-qr	Ratios for quarterly analysis
Ratio-yg	Graphs for annual ratio analysis
Ratio-yr	Ratios for annual analysis trends

Recommended literature

Andersen, Uffe: *Strategiens Økonomi*, CBS Press, Copenhagen, 1997.

Cohn, Theodore and Roy A. Lindberg: *Survival and Growth*. Amacon, 1974.

Flamholtz, Eric and Ellen Cook: *Connotative Meaning and its Role in Accounting Chance*, Accountings, Organisations and Society Vol. 3 no. 2, 1978.

Gordon L.A., D.F. Larcker & F.D. Tuggle: *Strategic Decision Process and The Design of Accounting Information Systems*. Conceptual Linkages AOS, Vol. 3, no. 3/4 p. 203 - 213, 1978.

Govindarajan V. and Anil K. Gupta: *Linking Control Systems to Business Unit Strategy*. Accountings, Organisations and Society. Vol. 10 no. 1, 1985.

Hartmann Stig: *Strategic accounting or accounting strategy*. An empirical investigation of the relationship between strategic management and management accounting. Institut for informatik og regnskabsvæsen, Copenhagen Business School, 1993.

Hill Charles W.L. and Gareth R. Jones: *Transaction cost analysis and strategy - structure choice*, Strategic Management Journal, Vol. 9, 159 - 172, 1988.

Holmes G. and Sugden A., *Interpreting Company Reports and Accounts*, Woodhead-Faulkner 4th ed., 1990.

Horovitz Jacque and Jean-Pierre Pitol-Belin: *Stratégie pour la PME*, McGraw-Hill, 1986.

Johannsen-Duus Henrik: *Strategisk ledelse af innovationsprocesser*. Thesis for Afsætningsøkonomisk Institut, Copenhagen Business School, 1993.

Johnsen Erik: *Introduktion til Ledelseslære*, CBS Press Copenhagen, 1982.

Johnsen Erik: *Strategisk Analyse og Syntese*. CBS Press Copenhagen, 1993.

Jørgensen, Kj.A., *Strategisk ledelse i mellemstore virksomheder*. Industrirådet, Kbh., 1997.

Kaplan R.S. & A.A. Atkinson: *Advanced Management Accounting*. 2nd Edition, Prentice Hall, 1989.

Kirkegaard Henning: *Rebuskonceptet*. Civiløkonomernes Forlag, Copenhagen, 1987.

Lucas, H.C., *Information systems concepts for management*, Auckland, McGraw-Hill 2nd ed., 1982.

Merten Hans-Lothar: *Die Pleitemacher*. Verlag Moderne Industri, 1975.

Ohmae, K., *Den strategiske hjerne*. Schultz, Kbh., 1986.

Porter M. E., Competitive Advantage: *Creating and Sustaining Superior Performance*. The Free Press, N.Y., 1985.

Rappaport, Alfred: *Creating Shareholders' Value*. The Free Press, A Division of Macmillan Inc., New York, 1986.

Simmonds K: *Strategic Management Accounting*, Management Accounting, Vol. 59, no. 4 pp. 26 - 29, 1981.

Sveriges Rationaliseringsförbund: *Kapitalrationalisering*. Liber, Stockholm, 1982.

Thorisson, G.P., og Karlsson, B.G., *Lykiltölur*, Framtíðarsýn ehf., 1996.

Waterhouse J.H. and P. Tiessen: *A Contingency Framework for Management Accounting Systems Research*. Accounting, Organisations and Society, Vol. 3 no. 1, 1978.

Wilson, B., *Systems- Concepts, Methodologies and Applications*, John Wiley & Sons, 1984.

Index